T0207612

Why *A Proven Bridge over Troubled Waters* Is a Must-Read ...

"*A Proven Bridge over Troubled Waters* is a must-read for everyone. Val McCray is a most powerful writer who prayerfully listens to the voice of God and lets her fingers do the writing. This book will surely encourage you when the storms of life are raging. The words of the Lord will give you hope just when you think you are down for the last count. It even speaks prophetically to personal situations one may be dealing with at that time. This book is exactly what the world needs. I'm looking forward to the next 'best thing' the Lord will speak through this powerful woman of God."

—T. Wright, president and founder, Mending Bridges, Humble, Texas

"Oh, how I can hear the Lord speaking to you! I thank him for using you, because you truly encourage me."

—R. Richardson, Rochester, New York

"Reading Val McCray's encouraging words is one of the highlights of my daily quiet time. I look forward each morning to reading it, and I am always blessed. Some days, it seems the message is custom tailored just for me based on something I have been through, am going through, or am about to experience. I love the simplicity and clarity of Val's writing style because it is always real, raw, relevant, and reassuring. She has a blessed pen, and by using it, she's walking in her gift and being a blessing to everyone who reads her work."

—J. Anderson-Blair, Missouri City, Texas

"Thank you so much for these encouraging messages! You are such a gifted and anointed writer!"

—R. Franklin, Houston, Texas

"I am going to have to refer to you as my minister to women, who through you and your writings can find Jesus and begin to read and understand the Bible as I am so learning from you. I thank you for you and for all the prayers. May God continue to use you to help others as you are so helping me right now. Val, you are truly a blessing from God. I am so blessed to be a part of your ministry. Thank you so very much!"

—S. Doucet, Houston, Texas

"We are honored and humbled to receive what God has given you to share with His people!"

—E. Johnson-Rouzan, Houston, Texas

"Oh, Val! Bless you, bless you, and bless you. How amazing that you sometimes just grab and shake me through these e-mails. Praise God for your encouraging words. You are our vessel. Thank you, thank you, and thank you."

—F. Williams, Houston, Texas

"This uplifted me in so many ways. I sure hope you're saving these for your family. Such a legacy of memories."

—R. Thompson, Houston, Texas

"What a joy and a blessing it is to have such a special gift that you share with others. Continue to allow the Lord to lead and guide you in a mighty way. Bountiful blessings to you and happy birthday to your mom, who is praising and uplifting his holy name! Love you, my sister in Christ."

—V. Robinson, Houston, Texas

"Your gift with the written word is a blessing to many. So much that I have in my heart about my own mother who transitioned last year is expressed in your writings. Blessings to you."

—R. Barlow, Houston, Texas

"It's amazing, Val McCray, that you have the gift to bring such things back to life, and give your audience a glimpse of hope and how to celebrate those special loved ones who have transitioned to glory."

—D. Dobbins, Boston, Massachusetts

"You've done it again! Always on time with the encouraging words ... tears are falling, and I just want to say thank you in the name of Jesus!"

—P. Morrow, Houston, Texas

A PROVEN
BRIDGE
–OVER–
TROUBLED
WATERS

*A Compilation of Encouraging Words to Help Carry You
Over When You Feel Like Life Is Trying to Take You Under*

VAL McCRAY

A PROVEN BRIDGE OVER TROUBLED WATERS
A COMPILATION OF ENCOURAGING WORDS TO HELP CARRY YOU OVER WHEN YOU FEEL LIKE LIFE IS TRYING TO TAKE YOU UNDER

iUniverse books may be ordered through booksellers or by contacting:

iUniverse
1663 Liberty Drive
Bloomington, IN 47403
www.iuniverse.com
1-800-Authors (1-800-288-4677)

Scripture quotations marked NLT are taken from the Holy Bible, New Living Translation, copyright 1996, 2004, 2007. Used by permission of Tyndale House Publishers, Inc. Carol Stream, Illinois 60188. All rights reserved.

Scripture quotations marked NIV are taken from the Holy Bible, New International Version. NIV. Copyright 1973, 1978, 1984 by International Bible Society. Used by permission of Zondervan. All rights reserved.

Scripture quotations marked KJV are from the Holy Bible, King James Version (Authorized Version). First published in 1611. Quoted from the KJV Classic Reference Bible, Copyright 1983 by The Zondervan Corporation.

ISBN: 978-1-5320-0911-2 (sc)
ISBN: 978-1-5320-0912-9 (e)

Library of Congress Control Number: 2016920990

Print information available on the last page.

iUniverse rev. date: 2/10/2017

Train up a child in the way he should go: and when
he is old, he will not depart from it.
—Proverbs 22:6

This book is written and dedicated to the memory of my
parents, Deacon and Mrs. Roy L. McGruder.

July 3, 1935–August 10, 2012
October 8, 1945–December 16, 2012

Even through death, you teach us about life, and
for every lesson … we do thank you!
—Rod, Vince, Val, and Kim

Contents

Foreword

It was Job who stated in chapter 14, verse 1, that "Man that is born of a woman is of a few days and full of trouble." Being married to Val McCray has been quite an adventure. Our journey together these past seven years has brought us both great joy and great pain. However, no matter the circumstances of our lives (e.g., death on both sides of the family, planting and pastoring a church, blending families, and so on), we have always been grateful for the abundant grace of God, even during our darkest hours.

This book, *A Proven Bridge over Troubled Waters*, will prove to be just as the writer of Hebrews said, an "anchor for your soul" (Hebrews 6:19). My wife invests great time in fellowship and prayer with our Lord and Savior Jesus Christ, and this book was birthed out of her very own personal encounters with God and challenges of this life.

No matter what your current situation or challenge may be, please read this book with an open heart and mind as well as the awareness that the woman who wrote it is indeed a living testimony to the sustaining power of grace and hope found only in the Lord Jesus Christ. Blessings on you!

—Dr. Clyde W. McCray, husband and pastor, Bethel
Missionary Baptist Church, Houston, Texas

God-given talents and ordained missions granted to His children often yield amazing results that may be misunderstood by those who are apart from Him. It is with this thought in mind that I address the work of this author. As children, we don't know where God will lead us or what we will experience along life's journey, but as we grow in His grace and His wisdom, we begin to learn to trust Him and follow His leadings unquestioningly. Blind faith and dedication to what He has in store for us will leave an indelible mark on our lives and the lives of our loved ones.

This work is the direct result of following God even under sometimes difficult circumstances. It represents the heart of the author as He speaks to her daily. In an effort to encourage herself, the author encourages those around her to believe in Him and to believe that He will always deliver His children from the furnaces of life in which we often find ourselves. Each piece of this work represents an amazing encounter with our Lord and Savior that will encourage you to move to another level in your faith. Each piece, while separate, weaves an amazing spiritual quilt that will encourage believers to seek the *cover* of His word.

I pray God's rich blessings upon Sister McCray and all of those who read this anointed work.

—Dr. Cheryl McGruder-Holloway, retired educator,
Bradenton, Florida (aunt of the author)

Acknowledgments

Lord, I thank You for once again being faithful to Your word. You continue to allow my gifts to make room for me and bring me into the company of great people; this book is evidence of that. I am forever humbled and honored that You continue to use me in Your service. Thank you, Sir.

To my husband and pastor, Dr. Clyde W. McCray, with my whole heart, I thank you for your consistent love and support. You have always supported me in whatever I have put my hands to, and for that, I am eternally grateful. You are truly a man after God's own heart, and your Christian walk exemplifies that daily. I cannot imagine life without your guiding hand of love and patience. Regardless of how busy you are, I am always the priority. You take the time to hear my every concern. I pray that the anointing of the Most High God will continue to overshadow you as His greatness continues to reign in your life, your ministry, and our marriage.

To my siblings, I love you guys in a mad-crazy kind of way! We have truly learned firsthand that God really is a proven bridge over troubled waters. Having to bury Daddy and Mama in just four short months was indeed our greatest test to date, and it is only by the amazing grace of God that we are still standing. My love and support for you guys is always and forever. Every word that has been penned on these pages has been done with you all in mind. My prayer is that this book will minister to your soul as you read it just as much as it ministered to mine while I was writing it.

Demika, Merneen, Reta, and Sylvia, you sisters are truly over the top! God really did something special when He ordained our bond of sisterhood. You are such spiritual powerhouses in your own areas of giftedness, and I glean from you every chance I get. You were there when Daddy died and then when Mama died. And to think we met by chance. I chuckle over the fact that all of this greatness began with Merneen complimenting my shoes in Luby's Cafeteria one afternoon. That meeting was divine intervention for such a time as this. When I couldn't pray, y'all prayed for me. When I had to cry, y'all cried with me. No strings attached and no questions asked. The fresh anointing of God is truly amazing. Thank you all for wailing on the wall for me at a time when I needed it the most. It really did save my life.

To my Bethel church family, the bond that we share is a very rare yet phenomenal one. You all are always there to support Pastor and me in every way. You are a very spiritually unique people. When Pastor receives a vision or an instruction from the Lord, you roll up your sleeves and go to work without complaining or murmuring. Many times, we have had to encourage one another along the way, but then that is what families do. We are small, but we are strong. You are definitely a Nehemiah 4:6 group, for you truly have a mind to work. I release much love and blessings to each of you.

Real Praying Mothers, thank you for your prayers, encouragement, and support. Serving as your intercessor has been an eternally gratifying experience. To my social media family, thank you all so much for receiving these words and encouraging me with your own. We serve an amazing God, and I give Him all the praise for this magnificent gift He has given me. So many times when you responded to the daily words of encouragement, I could literally see your hearts smiling because of the encouragement you received that helped to provide direction for your way. I pray God's very best for you as you continue to seek Him for all things.

Finally, to my daughter, Kyndahl, you inspire me in ways that you don't even understand right now. Being your mom has helped to mature my walk with the Lord. You are already a powerful vessel for God, and I know that your future is bright and filled with good success. I can already see Him performing a mighty work in you, and I love watching you mature into a beautiful butterfly. You are a leader among leaders because God says so. The best is yet to come for you, and just remember that Mom, Pas, and your dad will always love and support you.

Introduction

Storm clouds! They form in all our lives. Regardless of lifestyle, race, education, or socioeconomic background, storms will come. They invade your personal life, your professional life, and, yes, even your spiritual life. However, as you are faced with them, having someone to encourage you as you go through them is priceless. Encouragement is something all of us need and at some point desire. For me, encouraging others is like breathing. In other words, it comes so naturally that sometimes I don't even realize the magnitude of the gift myself. Simply put, I love God and I love people. The impact of being able to talk with someone who has actually been through a storm that you are currently going through is invaluable. I am a true witness and real live testimony of God's forgiveness and His faithfulness. Over the years, I have been afforded the wonderful opportunity to meet and share with many people through the word of God, using my very own personal stories of tragedy and triumph. I am indebted to the Lord for allowing me to help others get through their own tests and trials. Undeniably a product of the prayers of the righteous, I readily admit that without prayer, my life would be in a continual state of calamity. I am grateful to God for allowing me to hail from such a rich line of prayer warriors and Bible teachers. I consistently encourage others to stand firm in the knowledge of who they are in Christ and what His word says about them. In order to do this, one must first learn the word and then develop a love for it. When you fall in love with the word, you will have no problem obeying the word, and when you follow this pattern, positive change will manifest in your life.

I believe that God created every man, woman, boy, and girl with a specific purpose and destiny. We all have divine callings in our lives. Part of my calling is to pass the torch of experience through encouragement and wisdom to those who are traveling the road behind me. How long one lives is not nearly as important as how *well* one lives. Therefore, I simply encourage others to live their best lives, according to divine biblical principles. There is no other book that can and will impact your life like the Holy Bible. It is the driving force behind a life of true success. Learning and living the word of God will provide you with a sound mind, harmony, wisdom, and peace.

Although I have been walking with the Lord for many years now, I am the first to admit that I have endured many storms, made countless mistakes, and suffered great heartache and pain along the way. However, through all the ups and downs, hills and valleys, detours and exits of life, I have indeed learned that God really is a keeper of His word. He is faithful, forgiving, and patient. Regardless of where you are in life right now, keep in mind that every day is a day of thanksgiving when you know the Lord. Therefore, I encourage you to never give up, because God's compassions fail not and His mercies are new every morning. In addition, I further encourage you to practice obedience, loving, and forgiveness every day, for obedience frees the spirit, love frees the heart, and forgiveness frees them both.

Whether you are currently in the middle of a midnight-hour experience, enjoying a gumbo life, or living life responsibly, this book is for you. If you are in any way unsure about the ground on which you currently stand, this book is for you. Why? Because each of these very practical and personal messages has been written based solely on the word of God and is easy to read and digest. I truly believe that iron does sharpen iron. Therefore, I invite you to take this very critical, yet sometimes comical, journey with me as we encourage one another in the Lord.

Well, the vision has been written, and the time has come for it to speak. I encourage you to read it with an open heart and mind as I prove to you that God really is a *proven* bridge over troubled waters!

—Valandia M. McCray

A Midnight-Hour Experience
(Romans 8:26–28)

It's late at night, and you can't sleep. It's been a rough week. It seemed like everything that could go wrong did go wrong. You turn on the television, and nothing holds your attention, so you turn it off. You get up and walk through the house, making sure all is well. The entire family is sleeping soundly. All seems to be well on the outside, but a troubling undercurrent deep within you tells quite a different story. For days now, your spirit has been so heavy, but you don't know why. You feel prompted that something is about to happen, but you don't know what. You decide to go back to bed since all is quiet and still. Finally, you get back out of bed and go down on your knees to tell God about what you are feeling, but nothing comes out but a flood of tears. Ever been there? I surely have.

One thing I love about the Holy Spirit is He never allows anything to take us by surprise. He has implanted within each of us a discerning spirit. The interesting thing about life is none of us are exempt from trouble. Regardless of our financial status, our Ivy League education, the neighborhood we live in, or the position of influence we hold on elite boards or in the church, life happens to all of us. In the classroom setting, the teacher teaches the lesson and then issues the test. However, on the stage of life, the Lord issues the test and then teaches the lesson. Interesting, huh? Jesus advises us in James 1:2–3 to count it all joy when we face various tests and trials, because eventually they will indeed produce patience in our lives. When you have discerning moments of something unsettling in your spirit, stop and acknowledge them to the Lord. The most wonderful thing about the Lord is when I cannot find the words to express to Him what I am feeling, the Holy Spirit steps in and gives meaning to each tear that falls from my eyes. He loves His children that much. Your IQ has nothing to do with this because this is all about the spiritual. In life, a translator serves as a bridge of communication between two sides. Well, the Holy Spirit serves as a divine translator of all spiritual matters. He lovingly ministers to the ache in your soul, and then carries the true meaning of what's really going on directly to the Father without you ever having to utter a word. Oh, how I love it! Sometimes all we can do is cry, but there is great consolation in knowing that the Lord cherishes every one of our tears and in turn uses them to water the soil of our hearts. In exchange for my spirit of heaviness, He clothes me with a garment of praise!

Today, I encourage you not to be so hard on yourself if you cannot put your words together. Go ahead and cry if you must, but then allow the Lord to redress you and proceed to get your praise on. Remember He is the crème de la crème of navigational systems in that He knows exactly where you are and what's going on. You may be going through a difficult and devastating period in your life right now, but I invite you to join me in remembering His promise that all things will work together for your good because you love Him and are called according to His purpose.

I stand in agreement with you today, for there is power in agreement.

All Rise! Court Is Now in Session
(Revelation 12:9–11)

"All rise! Court is now in session." This is a command every one of us has been issued at least once in our lives. Whether it was traffic court, criminal court, civil court, or divorce court, we have all had to heed this command. It does not matter if you were there personally to handle a matter or simply to support a friend; when the judge enters the courtroom, you must obey this command to rise or you are out of order with possible consequences to follow. Regardless of your level of importance in society, in a trial setting, you are one of two people: the plaintiff or the defendant. The pretrial setting goes something like this. The officer of the court is present to read a docket, which consists of the names of people who must appear before a judge for a particular reason. There are attorneys present to represent both sides. The court reporter is present. Finally, once all parties are ready to proceed, the judge enters the courtroom. The "All rise" command is issued. Your name is called. You come forward with your legal representation and stand before the judge to hear the charges that have been brought against you. You enter a plea of guilty or not guilty, and depending on your response, you are given the option of a trial by jury or a trial by judge. You are then provided enough time to prepare your case along with a date on which to reappear in court. Get the picture? Does this sound familiar?

As children of God, we are constantly on trial because of charges being levied against us by Satan. The scriptures remind us in Revelation 12:9–11 that he is an accuser of the brethren. It may be our character, reputation, our integrity—or all three at the same time. However, it really doesn't matter; the point is Satan is always behind it. As he roams the earth, he has developed a well-deserved reputation for being the one who seeks to devour the believer through the meticulous process of stealing, killing, and destroying. His game is tight. His goal is on point. He has one directive in mind, and just like a laser of light, he zeros in on his target and will not stop until his goal is met. The stage is set, and the accusations have been made. The time has come to appear in court. Satan proudly enters the courtroom and takes his seat to the left of the bench, as he is sure that his case against you is airtight, because after all, you did commit the sin. You enter the courtroom and take your seat, not real sure as to how things will turn out, depending on your level of spiritual maturity. Satan knows you are nervous because he sees it all over you. He is elated because he is confident that he has destroyed yet another soldier on the front lines of the battlefield.

Now comes the game changer as everybody hears the command, "All rise! Court is now in session ... the Honorable Judge God the Father presiding!"

The judge calls you forward and reads the charges that have been brought against you. Satan chuckles again, because after all, you did commit the act. The judge then asks if you have legal representation, and before you can respond, Jesus enters the courtroom and proudly identifies Himself as the attorney for the defense! The plot thickens as the tables have just turned. Satan is now the one who is aggravated, as Jesus is positioned to the right of the judge's bench. The judge then asks the question, "Jesus, how does Your client plead?"

Jesus replies, "Not guilty, Your Honor, by way of redemption!"

Not only does Jesus enter a plea for you, but He specifically requests that all charges be dropped due to insufficient evidence provided by the accuser. That's right! Because you have repented and asked for forgiveness, the Lord has granted you a pardon and your record has been wiped clean. Therefore, because of the lack of evidence, the judge agrees and drops all charges against you. Satan is fuming but must concede because no evidence can be found.

You have been given the victory through the blood of Jesus once again! Hallelujah to the Lamb of God for the blood that covers all sins. As the song says, "What can wash away my sins? Nothing but the blood of Jesus?" Thank God for the blood.

Are You a Seasoned Saint?

(Matthew 5:13–16)

I love hanging out with the girls. It's time well spent doing all the things that girls do—no husbands, no children, and no to-do lists, just us girls having our own kind of fun. For weeks, you chat and e-mail in excitement leading up the big day because it's one that you very rarely get between home, work, church, and so on. You may start out at breakfast, and then the real fun begins. First up is some serious shopping. You all are going from one store to another, trying on clothes, getting one another's opinions as you buy clothes, shoes, perfume, and everything else (you know … girl stuff). Now, everybody is starving for something good to eat. This is where things get tricky because everybody has to agree on where to eat. One wants seafood, another wants steak, and somebody else wants chicken. Finally, after plenty of discussion, you make a decision on where to go.

You get to the restaurant, and immediately, while laughing and talking in the parking lot, an aroma takes complete control of your senses. Everybody is talking about how good something smells while at the same time wondering what it is! Already starving, immediately, somebody says, "Whatever that is, that's what I'm having!"

As soon as you walk into the restaurant, somebody asks the waiter about the aroma, and he proudly boasts about it being the restaurant's top seller, which is the marinated and slow-roasted pork loin. Before he can even finish explaining what comes with it, somebody says, "I'm having the pork loin!"

You all have been seated and had your order taken. The good conversation and laughter continues to fill the air. At last, the food has arrived, and everybody is talking about how good their food looks and smells. Each of you is bragging about the presentation and how well everything is arranged on the big, beautiful plates. Now, finally, you are about to eat what has taken complete control of your senses and held them hostage for about forty-five minutes only to discover that what smelled so good and looked so good is really kind of tough and not even seasoned all that well.

Is this the disappointment others feel when they encounter you? Was it all really just a show? Here's the question child of God, are you really a seasoned saint, or do you just smell like one?

Authenticity
(Matthew 15:8)

Some time ago, my husband and I were having a conversation that reminded me of an experience I had while living in our former house. He and I were standing outside, saying good-bye to some friends when all of a sudden, I noticed how something had moved in my presence. I could not actually see what it was, but I did notice the movement of it. As I became more intrigued by whatever this was that was moving around me, I must admit I also became a little fearful simply because I could not see it. I stood still, took a deep breath, and calmed myself. It was then that I noticed a lizard on my garage door. All of a sudden, the lizard quickly ran from the garage door to the side of the house and from the side of the house to the hedges. After finally being able to zero in on what it was that was disturbing me, I then began to follow this lizard's every move.

All of a sudden, something dawned on me. Every surface this lizard landed on, it took on the same color as that object. I was totally shocked as my husband calmly explained to me that this lizard was known as a chameleon. After hearing this, I began to wonder to myself, "How many of us who say we believe the word of God and say we live for Him are really nothing more than *spiritual chameleons*?" We are always in the house with hands lifted up and mouths filled with praise, but our hearts are far from God! In Matthew 15:8 (KJV), the Lord says, "This people draweth nigh unto me with their mouth, and honoureth me with their lips; but their heart is far from me." How many of us are in this group that the Lord is speaking of?

Are the children of God guilty of looking one way while in the house of God or around the people of God but then looking totally different when in another setting? Do we really possess a Christlike identity, or are we nothing more than one who just changes with the surroundings? When you are a chameleon, you take on the identity of whatever setting you are in at the time as opposed to having an identity of your own. When you take on someone else's identity, you begin to look, think, and act like that person, not because of what's on the inside of him or her but because of what's on the inside of you!

If you are filled with uncertainty about who you are, it will show up. If you are the slightest bit double-minded in any area of your life, your instability will show up. As stated previously, when you discern a particular spirit about something or somebody, stand still, breathe, and gather yourself. Trust me when I say God will not allow His children to be ambushed by the enemy. We must totally trust Him to expose the truth about those situations and people that are troubling to us. God created every living thing, even the chameleon. However, it is sad commentary that chameleons exist in the form of people, and it's even worse to be one of them.

Today, I encourage you to be authentic not only in the eyes of people but most important in the eyes of the Lord. Don't allow someone else's way of thinking to become yours. God has given each of us a perfectly good working mind of our own. Besides, when you seek to emulate those around you, you in essence say to God that He made a mistake in the way He created you. The Bible teaches us in Psalm 139:14 that we are fearfully and wonderfully made in the image of God. When we embrace this biblical truth, we will become exactly who God intended for us to be without compromise of any kind. So you see, there really is no need to try to be like anybody else. You are perfect just the way you were created—in the image of God.

Bag Lady
(Proverbs 4:23)

I have always loved the smooth, eclectic sound of Erykah Badu. In my opinion, she is quite talented in the area of combining truth and wisdom for the purpose of reminding women everywhere of the dangers of carrying too much baggage. In this particular song, "Bag Lady," Erykah stresses to women the need for them to "pack light," because carrying too much baggage can be detrimental to their bodies, minds, and spirits. Some time ago, I was asked to be the speaker for an afternoon tea at a church here in the Houston area. The theme was "What's in Your Bag?" and what a time we had with this one. As I began to share with the ladies, I could quickly tell that many of them were guilty of carrying a great deal of baggage. The first and most common indicator was the tense body language. While they may have begun the afternoon on a light and friendly note, as the dialogue got underway, a number of them became somewhat quiet and reserved. The fact is excess baggage can and will cause you to miss out on the finer things that God has predestined for you. All too often, we allow ourselves to become preoccupied with junk. This is precisely why we are reminded in Proverbs 4:23 that we are to guard our hearts with all diligence.

So what's weighing you down? Are you still angry about the divorce? Or maybe you are still bitter about not getting the promotion? Are you secretly jealous of the one who did get the promotion? All of these behaviors are what I personally call toxic contaminants. A toxic contaminant is very powerful and has the ability to pollute or poison anything and everything in its path. If we are not prayerful about the baggage in our lives, our hearts can become contaminated, which in turn leads to a contaminated spirit and attitude. At the onset of my presentation, to generate a thought-provoking discussion, I placed several questions on the table for the women to ponder for a moment. My sole purpose for doing this was to guide us to the point of learning the true condition of our hearts through self-introspection. The Bible teaches us in Jeremiah 17:9 that the heart is deceitful and desperately wicked. Every person is a product of his or her life experiences. Therefore, we must take extra precaution against our hearts becoming deceitful and wicked.

Did you know that people can get to know you quite well and never hold a conversation with you? All it takes is careful and consistent observation. If anger is deeply rooted in your heart, it will certainly come out of your mouth. "Packing light," as Erykah says, is essential for every believer. We must learn how to release those things that weigh us. Holding on to the negative can affect our ability to soar through life like an eagle. We must rid ourselves of those things (and people) that prohibit us from being able to run the race of life with patience. We must discard anything from our lives that causes us to grow weary and faint while on our journey to healing and wholeness. God wants nothing but the best for His children, but we too must want it.

So what's it going to be? Will you continue to struggle with all those bags that weigh you down, or will you release them and begin to walk upright freely? As always, the choice is yours.

Bargain Basement Deals

(Isaiah 55:7–11)

All of my adult life, I have been a shopper. I love beautiful things that are of excellent quality. However, anything can be beautiful on the surface, but the true quality of it can only be found on the inside. When I was in my tenacious twenties, my girlfriends and I would hear about bargain basement sales at various stores. We would saddle up, gas up the vehicle, and get some breakfast. After we completed all the preliminaries, we would then run all over town in hopes of finding what we thought would be some of the greatest deals. At the end of the day, I would return home with a bunch of stuff I really didn't need, but because it was considered to be a good deal, I had bought it. Ooh, this is so dangerous!

Many people like me have been guilty of chasing after what they *think* is a good deal or a good catch. Satan is so subtle and clever that he can place something right in our path, and just like that, we take the bait. However, as you grow stronger and wiser in the word of God, you will begin to pay closer attention to the subtle tricks and traps of the enemy, especially in the world of words. God's children don't have to chase after a good deal or a good catch. Not only does our Father in heaven own the earth and everything in it, but He also has total control of it all. In addition, we certainly don't have to go to the lowest levels to get it. Did you catch that? The basement is the lowest level. Why in God's name do we go shopping around, looking for what we think is the good stuff at the lowest level possible? Even in some of the most critical areas of life, we are guilty of seeking out what we think is the best of something in the low places. Someone once said, "Quality doesn't go on sale," and this statement is loaded with truth.

Many believers have allowed themselves to become hoodwinked and bamboozled by the enemy. Satan has a way of causing us to think that time is running out on us. This misguided thought causes many believers to rush to judgment in making major decisions that can and will forever change the course of their lives. Many have done this in the area of employment and ended up miserable. Some of us have done this in the area of buying a home that ended up in foreclosure, thus ruining our credit for a season. It has even been done in the area of love, causing marriages to end in divorce with children in tow.

The prophet Isaiah reminds us in Isaiah 55:7–9 that God's thoughts for our lives far outweigh our own. He even has precise times in which He will answer our prayers. But are we praying about these things, or are we just moving on what we think or feel is best for us? God sees and knows the big picture of our lives. In other words, His panoramic view has a panoramic view. We can only see a portion. Therefore, it is always to our advantage as children of God to trust in Him with all our hearts and lean not to our own understanding (Proverbs 3:5–6). He has promised to direct our path if we acknowledge Him in all our ways. God is a keeper of His word. He is faithful to deliver on every promise that He makes. In fact, Isaiah 55:11 confirms this by declaring that God's word will not go out and return void, but it will accomplish that which He pleases and prosper in the thing He sent it out to do. So today, I encourage you to simply trust God. I further encourage you to develop a *believe God* attitude.

Got a big decision to make? Pray, wait, and listen. Brothers, are you thinking about asking that sister to marry you? Pray, wait, and listen. Thinking about accepting the job offer? Pray, wait, and listen. You want the house really bad? I strongly advise you to pray, wait, and listen. Considering starting a business? Pray, wait, and listen. Saints, God does want us to have the very best, but it must be done in His time and according to His plan. Don't ever forget the words of the church elders: "He may not come when you want Him, but He's always right on time!"

Remember, saints, for the children of God, there are no deals to be found in low places.

Be a Conduit and Not a Reservoir
(Romans 15:1–5)

We all have people in our lives we love to see come; at the same time, we also have those we love to see go. Those whose company we enjoy the most tend to bring a particular flavor to the atmosphere. They bring the grace of a grateful spirit. They bring an aroma of freshness. Simply put, they bring *light*! They serve the universe in the capacity of conduits by allowing the Holy Spirit to freely flow through them. By example, they are the ones who don't allow life's challenges and dilemmas to rule their emotions and dictate their life. They enter a room and immediately change the energy of the entire room. They are the true power shifters of the world. Their influence is always positive. Their attitude is always upbeat. Do they have difficult days? Of course they do. However, they have a level of faith in God that has been tried, tested, and proven to be true upon which they depend. People always want to be in their company because just being in their presence provides the hope they so desperately need to never give up. Being in the company of a divine conduit helps to strengthen the faith of others.

Then there's the reservoir. Oh boy, the reservoir. A reservoir is a standing body of water that has no movement at all. Over time, it becomes stagnant and stale. The reservoirs are those people who have been damaged by life just as we all have, yet they have become bitter instead of better. Life's situations have caused their hearts to become callused in their concern for others. In other words, they have become hard-hearted toward anything or anybody who chooses to press their way amid life's test and trials. They fail to be of good cheer. Instead, they are negative and never have a kind word to offer. Ironically, they are guilty of residing in the downward flowing river of denial. Simply put, they have been damaged by life and are really crying out for help. This is where the conduit comes in. Romans 15:1–3 advises that those of us who are strong and able in the faith step in and lend a hand to those who falter and not just do what is most convenient for us. Strength is for service, not status. Each one of us needs to look after the good of the people around us. People are not down or bitter because they want to be. However, as Christians who are strong in the faith, it becomes our divine responsibility to look after those who are weak.

So the next time you see someone acting out, pull that person aside and ask him or her this simple question: "How can I help?" Pray for these people. Support them. Be that confidential listening ear they need. It may be their time today, but it could be yours tomorrow. I encourage you to always remember that life is like a Ferris wheel in that it keeps on turning. You may be up today, but only God knows what's coming tomorrow.

Becoming a Good Steward
(Luke 16:1—10)

Being thankful is about so much more than just saying thank you with your *lips*. It is really about saying thank you with your *life*! How many of us, if accused today, would be found guilty of being thankful? How many of us can honestly say we are good stewards? In order to declare someone guilty of being a good steward, one must do a comprehensive evaluation to account for how that person handles those things that have been placed in his or her care by someone else. Stewardship is an attitude. It comes from the root word *steward*, which means to be a property manager. In other words, regardless of what you may think, you are not the owner. You are simply the overseer of something that really belongs to somebody else. As children of God, we are mere stewards, but Christ is the owner of all things. Because of His love for us, He allows us to enjoy the abundant blessings of His property. Good stewardship is a sign of maturity. We must never allow ourselves to be guilty of begging God for new and improved blessings, knowing that we have not done all we can to maintain our current blessings. What do I mean? There are times when we petition God for a promotion when our attendance and job performance are poor on the job we currently have. In addition, there are others who constantly whine about a new car when the one they drive now is always dirty, in need of service, and in complete disarray. Why do we always want more when we are not good stewards over what we already have? If this is you, I strongly encourage you to make some changes.

In Luke 16, Jesus tells His disciples the story of a rich man who had a crooked manager who had been taking advantage of his position by running up huge personal expenses. So He called him on the carpet by saying to him, "What's this I hear about you? You're fired. And I want a complete audit of your books." Immediately, the manager went to work once again, trying to clean up the mess he had made, not realizing that he was digging an even deeper hole for himself.

How many of us are like this crooked manager? We must realize that God sees past appearances straight to the soul of who we really are. We may be able to fool people, but never God. Good stewardship is about walking in honesty and integrity. True integrity is doing the right thing even when no one is watching, and God rewards that. If you have been guilty of poor stewardship, then I encourage you to privately go before the throne of grace and seek forgiveness for your mishandling of matters. God is always ready to forgive His children of their wrongs and lovingly place them back on the right path. But acknowledgment is critical, simply because you cannot conquer what you are not willing to confront. Trust me when I say, you can deal with receiving a pink slip from people, but you never want to receive one from the Lord!

Conquering the Curse
(Luke 10:19)

In order to conquer anything, you must first be willing to confront it, and curses are no different. They too must be attacked head-on. Regardless of the nature of a curse, one is able to overcome it. A curse is nothing more than an appeal to a supernatural being for harm to come to somebody or something. Although there are many different kinds of curses, one thing they have in common is all of them cause harm. There is no such thing as a positive curse. Those who curse others not only harm their intended target; they also harm themselves.

Sometimes we are even guilty of cursing ourselves with the words from our own mouths. If you do not erect a spiritual wall of protection around yourself, the negative prayers of others can indeed bring harm to you. In fact, it may be happening to you right now. For the believer, God has provided us with the absolute greatest power to conquer any and all curses, and that power is prayer. Prayer, better known as spiritual warfare, can yield the greatest results against the principalities and powers of Satan. Sadly though, some of us still don't fully realize the powerful impact that our words have when it comes to setting things in motion. In order to gain power and strength, we must learn to pray constructive prayers with a repentant heart. The Bible teaches us in Psalm 66:18 that if we regard iniquity in our hearts, God will not hear our prayers. Iniquity is simply holding on to the junk we have in our hearts against other people. It is the secret stuff that nobody can physically see. However, God sees it all and He teaches us in Matthew 6:14–15 that if we forgive others who sin against us, then He will indeed forgive us of our sins. In order to conquer a curse, you must identify it and effectively take authority over it. Luke 10:19 reminds us that we have been given the power to tread on serpents and scorpions and over all the power of the enemy.

People curse others for many reasons. Most curses are fueled by jealousy, envy, anger, malice, hatred, bitterness, and so on. However, the word of God has the power to handle every one of them. Some people curse others out of ignorance. However, there are those who know exactly the impact that their words have and how they will affect others. This is why it is so critical that you pray in total alignment with God's word. You must learn to agree with Him on all matters. There is power in agreement, and again, you must protect yourself and your family daily.

So how do you wage war against a curse? You study the word and get to know what it says about you. Don't depend on someone else to study for you. You must allow it to become embedded in your spirit. You must learn to understand and appreciate your own spiritual power and strength. Knowing the word of God is so very necessary when it comes to fighting spiritual battles. In 2 Corinthians 10:4, it teaches us that we cannot fight a spiritual battle with a carnal weapon. In other words, in order to fight and win a spiritual battle against Satan, we must use the spiritual weapons that God has empowered us with, such as prayer and fasting. These are two of the most powerful weapons we have in our arsenal, and combined, they can destroy any curse that is formed against us. It doesn't matter what was done down through the family line. It can stop with you. However, you must make a conscious effort to search the scriptures for the purpose of learning how to stop the stronghold of curses on your life.

A stronghold is just simply something that has a *strong hold* on you. Just because your mother, grandmother, and great-grandmother may have done something does not mean that you will do it too. Just because Daddy was a rolling stone who fathered many pebbles doesn't mean you will be guilty of the same reckless behavior. Stop believing that garbage. The devil is a lie! In fact, he is the father of lies. Yes, generational curses are very real, but so is the spoken word of God. Hear it, learn it, do it, and watch Him bring you through it.

Remember, saints, "No weapon that is formed against you shall be able to prosper," according to Isaiah 54:17 (KJV). The Bible never says that a weapon would not be formed, but it does say that it will not prosper. Fight the good fight, saints!

Crock-Pot Lessons
(The Book of Proverbs)

My dear mother, who now rests with the Lord, used to tease me about being so organized. She would say, "Girl, you just have too many lists for me! A list for this and a list for that … You are just too doggone organized!" And then, of course, she would have a really good laugh at my expense! However, whenever someone needed to plan an event, she would quickly say, "Girl, call Val. She's the expert!" At one point, I became so inundated with planning events for other people that *my* family's schedule began to suffer. I must have order, or I simply cannot function. In my home, both of my offices, my car, whatever I am responsible for, there has to be order or things just don't seem to come together. Because I believe in family first, I make it a point to plan and post a meal calendar weekly. This simple act lifts a huge weight off of my shoulders. A new one is posted every Saturday so that my family will be fully aware of the coming attractions for next week's dinner. Between planning and cooking, reviewing calendars, running a smooth operation at home, wife duties, work duties, Mom duties, church duties, speaking engagements, girl time, encouraging words, and being a sister, an auntie, an intercessor, a confidante, a prayer partner, and so on, I sometimes get off track with my own personal eating schedule, and when this happens, things can get ugly. When I lose track of my routine eating schedule, not only do I become impatient, but I start eating all the wrong stuff and I immediately begin to feel the effects on my body. When my body becomes sluggish, I get grouchy, my patience gets short, and my attention span plummets.

For me, this downward spiral not only happens in the physical but also in the spiritual. When I don't get the proper amount of physical or spiritual nourishment, I become easily irritated and impatient. So I attempt to satisfy myself with something quick. Although we don't always realize it, many of us sometimes possess a microwave mentality, and this is not always healthy for the body or the soul. When I am too busy to sit down and spend quality time at the dinner table with my family, eating a healthy meal and conversing, that's a problem. When I don't get my daily dose of quiet time in the presence of the Lord, listening for His instructions, receiving His wisdom, that too is a problem. Whenever you get too busy for the Lord, trust me, you are too busy.

Many of us are guilty of not wanting to wait for anything. We want what we want when we want it and how we want it. However, Jeremiah 29:11 reminds us that God has a plan for each of our lives. Not only that, but He operates according to divine order. Because He is the master teacher, He knows precisely what lessons we need in order to become what we have been predestined to become before the world was ever formed. Some lessons are Crock-Pot lessons, and yet others are microwaveable. However, without a doubt, the Crock-Pot lessons carry the most value. Why? Because they come by way of the ongoing tests and trials for the purpose of marinating us to the point of developing a solid foundation of faith, hope, and trust in Him. As uncomfortable as they may be at times, the beauty of Crock-Pot lessons is that even though you must remain in the heat for a while, He will never allow you to burn. Not only that, but you will come out perfect and complete every time.

James reminds us that we are to count it all joy when we face various tests and trials, knowing that the trying of our faith will produce patience. There is no microwaveable way to develop faith, patience, or wisdom. Each of these virtues mature over time. God has a divine order for everything, according to Ecclesiastes 3, but sometimes we tend to have a "just nuke mine" mentality because we don't want to go through anything, and don't dare ask us to wait! However, being still and waiting on God to move is an excellent virtue. Is it difficult sometimes? Oh Lord, yes. But even in the toughest of times, we are reminded in Isaiah 41:10 that we don't have to be afraid, for He is with us. God confirms that He is our God and that He will strengthen and help us. So what additional assurance do we need? It may not always feel good to you, but I guarantee you when the Master declares you to be done, you will come out well seasoned, tender, and full of divine flavor every time.

Depression: The Silent Struggle
(Genesis 15, Jonah 4, 1 Kings 19)

Have you ever wondered just how many people who come to church week after week are struggling with depression? Although they are smiling on the outside, there is an undercurrent of something very different going on down inside. The sad reality is that on any given Sunday, the church can be referred to as the Broadway stage because of all the playacting that takes place. Reason being, we take great pride in dressing up the outside to look happy and content with life, when the reality is we are struggling incessantly on the inside. Yes, that's right. We may be dancing on the outside, while we are crying on the inside.

Depression is defined as a state of unhappiness and hopelessness. All of us, at some point or another, have experienced this very real and difficult emotion. But the good news is we are surrounded by good company. Often, as believers, although we may not always admit it, we sometimes tend to feel that we are the only ones who feel a certain way when that couldn't be further from the truth. The Bible mentions several great individuals who struggled with depression. Abraham, who was the father of the faith (Genesis 15); the prophet Jonah, who was disobedient to God's instructions to go to Nineveh to preach (Jonah 4); Elijah, who was known as God's boldest prophet (1 Kings 19); Saul, who served as Israel's first king (1 Samuel 16:14, 23); Jeremiah, who was known as the "Weeping Prophet" (book of Jeremiah); and of course we have Job, whose life consisted of one tragedy after another, yet he never turned his back on God. Each of these men shared one common bond in that God had a great call on their lives. And we are no different. Saints, anytime we are called to a great work, we will indeed suffer great difficulties that can lead into the valley of depression.

In today's society, depression can be brought by a medical diagnosis, a prolonged illness, the loss of a job, the death of a loved one, a divorce, shocking news, and so on. But the story doesn't have to end there. God does His best work in our lives when we are greatly challenged. When we are hard pressed, our prayer life improves. When we are challenged, our private time with the Father increases. When we are going through difficulty, our faith is strengthened. So you see, what you are experiencing is perfectly normal. In fact, it was King David who said, "I am troubled, I am bowed down greatly; I go mourning all the day long. I groan because of the turmoil of my heart" (Psalm 36:6, 8 NLT). Although depression may be the season you are in right now, it does not have to be your final sentence.

Through prayer, the study of God's word, being honest with yourself, and talking with other believers, you can overcome depression without fail. You must not allow depression to linger to the point of becoming a silent struggle for you. What you must do is sound the alarm, signaling to other believers that you are in need of some help. In 1 Corinthians 10:13 (KJV), the Bible reminds us, "No temptation has overtaken you that is not common to man. God is faithful, and He will not let you be tempted beyond your ability, but with the temptation He will also provide the way of escape, that you may be able to endure it."

Remember, saints, some of us are just coming out of the storm, others are about to go through the storm, and then there are those who are right in the eye of the storm. But none of us are exempt from the storm.

Distractions

(Psalm 46:10, 1 Thessalonians 4:11, Hebrews 4:11)

Are you so bogged down with life that it is a challenge to even hear from God? You get to bed late. You wake up early, and it seems like your spirit man never even rested in between. Life can be challenging to say the least. However, in order to create balance, we must make time to stop, look, and listen for God. Listening to God requires extreme effort and determination. However, learning to decipher the voice of God doesn't happen overnight. It takes time, energy, and effort on the part of the believer.

For those of us who walk with the Lord, there are times when we are so busy that it is a challenge just to hear what the Holy Spirit is saying to us. When this happens, it is imperative that we stop what we're doing, find a place to steal away for some solitude, and just listen. Just as with listening to the radio, we must work at finding the right channel that allows us to clearly hear from the Lord without all the static. Background noise comes in many forms, yet it only serves one purpose and that is to distract you from hearing what really needs to be heard. Background noise creeps in on the coattail of a busy lifestyle. It sometimes even infiltrates the spirit by way of those closest to us. Background noise is nothing more than another tactic the enemy uses to chip away at our fellowship with the Father. Background noise is what causes you to question God and doubt His love for you and what He has said. Background noise is what challenges your faith in His word. Background noise is what causes you to question His faithfulness to perform His word in your situation. But here's the thing. Psalm 46:10 instructs us to be still. First Thessalonians 4:11 instructs us to be quiet. Hebrews 4:11 instructs us to be diligent. Each of these instructions is given to prevent us from falling prey to the enemy.

Physical, mental, and emotional rest should be a priority with every believer. Why? Because, when we become tired, our resistance gets low, we become easily irritated, and the enemy has a greater chance of overtaking us. However, the word equips, empowers, and enables us to live a balanced life. Therefore, I encourage you to make it a priority to develop balance in your life. Seize every opportunity to rest physically, mentally, and emotionally so that you can become stronger spiritually. Busyness can be a distraction, and we must keep in mind that all *good* work ain't *God* work.

Begin each day with a promise to yourself: "Today, I will take time to rest. I will quiet my spirit man and allow him or her the opportunity to hear and to listen for what the Holy Spirit has to say. I will not become distracted by the distractions. I will simply allow him or her to be rejuvenated, revived, restored, and refreshed by the Master's presence." Then just do it.

Divine Diagnostics
(Philippians 4:6–8)

Have you ever had car trouble and were unable to locate the source of the problem? You tried this, and it didn't work. You tried that, and it didn't work. You continue to drive, and as you begin to pay closer attention to just how badly the car is running, you find yourself speculating about what you think the problem is. The fact is many of us dread the price we may have to pay to have a licensed specialist investigate and eventually diagnose the real issue under the hood. The problem has persisted and intensified so much that it has begun to affect other areas, causing them to become sluggish in one way or another. As a result, you finally decide to take the car to a professional to see what is really going on. However, before you could get the car in, the unthinkable happens. You find yourself broken down on the side of the road with your flashers on, signaling to the world you need help. How many of us are living life like this? How many of us have been trying to diagnose our own issues all because we don't want to pay the price to seek help from the licensed specialist? I know I have.

A diagnostic machine has the keen ability to investigate all the major components within a car's system for the purpose of seeing exactly where the problem is and resolving it. Well, for the believer, the word of God is that machine. However, we must be willing to connect ourselves to the word and remain there long enough for the Lord to reveal to us the truth about what is really ailing us. Since the deaths of my parents, only four months shy of each other, this is actually a pretty good description of where I find myself at times—sitting on the side of the road with my flashers on signaling "I need some help!" I truly thank God for the people He has placed in my life to recognize when my flashers are on and immediately come to my rescue.

Many called. Others came. But nevertheless, God used people to rescue me. Grief is a pretty strong emotion and a new territory for me. Some days are great, and others are a bit of a challenge. However, I know that the master mechanic knows just what I need in order to get back on the road. How we handle our lives can serve as a barometer for our level of spiritual growth and maturity. I don't profess to be Superwoman. When I need to talk, I talk. When I need to cry, I cry. Regardless of whether I am at home, in the office, or in the grocery store, emotionally speaking, if that is where I am at the time, that is what I do.

One of the biggest misconceptions about grief is it is only related to the loss of a loved one. Many people grieve the loss of a marriage or relationship, a job, or even a certain status in life they once enjoyed. Grief is grief. However, as I encourage myself, I also encourage you to go boldly to the throne of grace and lay out your situation before the Lord. Tell Him how you feel. Go ahead and cry on His capable shoulders. You must remember that He is ready, willing, and able to perfect those things that concern you, but you must invite Him into your situation. God loves you too much to just stand by and watch you become devoured by the anxieties of life. He has already provided you a way out, but whether or not you take it is totally up to you.

Divinely Downloaded Instructions
(Genesis 12:1–4)

Has the Lord ever downloaded an instruction into your spirit? If so, did you know it was Him? How did you respond? Did you immediately obey it, or did you debate it first? Did you share this experience with anybody, or did you keep it to yourself for fear of them thinking, *Well, you know?* I can recall the first time I heard the voice of God and how perplexed I felt. Before I came to know His voice, I used to wonder if I was losing it. There would be times during the day when seemingly out of nowhere, I would hear my name whispered in my right ear. Immediately, I would look over my shoulder for the person I just knew was playing a trick on me, but no one was there. As time passed, the voice became more persistent, and I began to hear it both in my quiet time and at night as I would try to sleep. At this point, I sensed that it was God so I politely asked Him to reveal Himself in a way that I could understand. The response came almost immediately. This powerful confirmation was crystal clear as His spoken word and His written word began to harmoniously blend in my spirit. This was exactly what I needed, and the peace I felt was just A-M-A-Z-I-N-G! Being able to discern the voice of God was a huge milestone. As a result, I began to record the dates and times that He would speak to me and what He would say. For years, He would speak to me between the hours of three and four in the morning. Whenever or whatever I was going through, the Lord would awaken me by whispering a scripture directly into my spirit. When I arose, I would routinely record the date and time. I listened as He spoke. What an experience.

Have *you* ever had an intimate encounter with God? How did it feel? Did you know that God speaks to His children? As believers, each of us is responsible for learning the voice of God in our lives. However, this will not happen until we completely surrender to Him. It takes getting off life's merry-go-round, turning off the TV, putting down the cell phone, and quieting yourself before Him in the spirit of total submission. This is very necessary if you are going to develop an intimate relationship with Him. God has deposited a wealth of greatness within you. However, in order to tap into it, you must position yourself to hear and receive His instructions. I am the first to admit that sometimes God's instructions seem to make no sense at all. However, when you've had enough encounters with Him, you don't ask questions. Instead, you just obey. God does not always explain Himself, and neither does He have to because He is sovereign. But keep in mind that real faith is being able to obediently carry out His instructions without a bunch of questions. You will not always understand why He instructs you to do some things, but I promise you, if you are obedient, the rewards are endless.

There have been times when the Lord has given me a word for someone, and when I am obedient, he or she is left staring at me in awe. On the flip side, there have been times when a complete stranger has shared a word with me that left me in complete awe. Some have wept … I have wept. Others were grateful … I too was grateful. For any challenge you will face in life, God has a solution, but you must allow Him a platform on which to speak to you. As you begin to walk in sync with the Lord, you will discover that His rewards for your obedience far outweigh the negative skepticism of people. Not everybody will receive your gift. However, the fact that God has given you the gift is confirmation that someone needs it. There are people in this world who need what only you can provide, but you must be obedient to His divine instructions. You only need to do what God instructs you to do. The story of Abraham in Genesis 12 is an excellent example of how obeying the voice of God will produce abundant blessings in your life.

So what divine instruction has God downloaded into your spirit? What has He told you to do, or where has He told you to go? Whom has He told you to minister to? What gifts have you been given to minister to others? The questions are endless, but then so are the blessings when you're obedient to His commands!

Emerging from the Ashes
(Isaiah 61:3)

Not too terribly long ago, I sincerely felt as though all hell was breaking loose in every area of my life. Have you ever felt like this? It seems as though once I got a handle on this, I was met with a challenge regarding that. Once things calmed down on the job, the embers rekindled themselves and shifted to the church. After successfully extinguishing the fire at the church, it quickly spread and began to rage at home. I remember saying, "My God, what is going on?" Then, of course, I was reminded of a time when the fires were raging in all places at the same time. Needless to say, I immediately became thankful!

Saints, sometimes we are guilty of focusing so much negative attention on the fire itself that we lose sight of its benefits. According to forest-fire experts, fire has the power to purify. It has the power to remove low-growing underbrush that will eventually create major problems on the surface. Fire has the ability to kill diseases that prey on trees, thus providing valuable nutrients to enrich the soil for new trees.

So what about the believer? Regardless of the situation, God has equipped each of His children with the necessary tools needed to emerge unscathed by the heated situations of life. Tests and trials purify us. They remove the low-growing underbrush in our lives that seeks to destroy the essence of who we are and what we believe as children of God. Tests and trials kill all those things that create disease in our lives and faith walk with the Lord. Through the prophet Isaiah, the Lord has promised to give us joy and gladness in the place of grief as well as a joyous praise in the place of mourning. Now who wouldn't want to make such an exchange? Through tests and trials, we become like strong trees that the Lord himself has planted. Divinely orchestrated challenges teach us perseverance. They challenge us not only to do better, but to be better.

Now, have you ever had a fire to rage out of control in your life seemingly destroying everything in its path? If a particular area in your life has been tested or destroyed by fire, the Lord wants to hear from you. He is waiting to lovingly provide you with the support needed to help you emerge from the ashes. He stands ready as the divine compass to guide you out of that place of ruin and to lead you into your new season. He wants to rebuild and recreate you. He seeks to restore you. He longs to revive you. He desires to refresh you.

Now that you know what He is willing to do to help you emerge from the ashes, what are you willing to do?

Giants in the Land
(1 Samuel 17)

Giants! We all have them. If you don't think you do, then I must inform you that one of yours may be denial. It has been said, the bigger they are, the harder they fall. But do they just fall? The answer is no. Instead, we must take them down. Your giant may not be the same as mine, and mine may not be the same as yours, but the fact is we all have them. Neither does it matter how well you may think you hide yours; I guarantee you someone has seen your giant rear its ugly head. Now, that person may not have admitted it to you, but trust me, he or she has seen it.

We all know the biblical story of David and Goliath, recorded in 1 Samuel 17. With five smooth stones and the Lord on his side, David was able to take down Goliath. Well, not only did he take down Goliath, but he also cut off his head. Now what does that say to the believer? It says that it is not enough just to take down our giant; we must cut off its head! If David had only taken Goliath down, once Goliath came to himself, he would have gotten back up again with an unspeakable fierceness. But because David cut off the head of the unconscious giant, that sealed any possibility of Goliath ever rising up against him again.

So here's the question: What giant has been haunting you? Is it that of unforgiveness, anger, bitterness, jealousy, or low self-esteem? Or maybe it's secret abuse, insecurity, guilt, shame, anxiety, self-pity, or something from your past that you just can't seem to shake. Whatever it is, it has consistently robbed you of your innermost personal peace and purpose. So, how do you take down your giant? Just as David did, the first thing you must do is prayerfully invite the Lord into your situation because the giant is way too big for you to handle. Then you must commit to being open and honest with the Lord. Doing this will immediately force you out of the window and into the mirror. The window allows you to focus on everybody else's giants, but the mirror reflects yours.

I can say without reservation that when you commit to focusing on the truth about who you are and what you have done, you are ready to face the giants of your past. Then, you can make peace with why the marriage really ended. Then, you can forgive yourself for aborting that baby twenty years ago or having a baby out of wedlock thirty years ago or dropping out of college or gambling away everything you and your spouse worked for or whatever the case may be. The point is that you must come clean before the Lord and allow Him to minister to you and love on you. His unconditional love and forgiveness sets the stage for you to forgive and release yourself. It is precisely at this point that you cut off the head of your giant and destroy it for good. So go ahead, empty yourself before the Lord and allow Him to set you free because, as the scripture says, "whom the Son sets free, is free indeed!" (John 8:36 KJV).

Gumbo Life
(Matthew 7:24–27)

My sister Kim makes a really good gumbo. She loads it up with shrimp, crab, sausage, and chicken, and when I tell you it's good ... believe it. I have never learned to make gumbo, and that's okay because I know that I can call on her to do it for me and she does it every time. I have enjoyed gumbo cooked many different ways with many different seasonings and ingredients; yet every person I have ever asked about preparing gumbo had one common thing to say, and that was the success is in the roux, or the foundation!

The year 2012 was indeed my toughest year to date. For me, it brought with it a good balance of tests and trials, ups and downs, laughter and sorrow, sunshine and rain, successes and failures. It was chock-full of questions like "How, God?" and even more questions of "Why, God?" It even brought out the truth about some "smiling faces" that were hidden in my camp. One of the most common questions I asked myself throughout 2012 was "God, how did I miss that? How did I not know?" Through my experiences, I was gently reminded that God does not reveal anything until we are ready to receive it. I have come to know that revealing something at the wrong time can be disastrous, to say the least. For that divine epiphany, I am thankful.

It is safe to say that life for me in 2012 was indeed a gumbo life! Just as with any good gumbo, the roux of a good life is the word of God. In Matthew 7:24–27 (NLT), the Bible teaches us about the wise man and the foolish man. The wise man who builds his house upon the rock is totally prepared when the storms and winds of life begin to blow. However, the house of the foolish man is destroyed at the slightest bit of wind and rain because he has not built his house on the foundation of God's word. We are no different.

Our ability to stand the tests and trials of life depends solely on how firm our foundation is. If our foundation is faulty, then our house will not stand.

Just as with a good gumbo, real living begins with getting the word down on the inside and allowing it to simmer a bit. As it begins to flavor you, the time comes to stir in some of your more critical ingredients, such as faith, obedience, patience, and forgiveness. You will quickly discover that you are creating quite a flavorful base as your aroma begins to change. Of course, none of this would be possible without a little heat or a few challenges because they help to tenderize you and produce the aroma. Now that you have a pretty good base simmering with the assistance of some heat, it's time to add some love, joy, peace, long-suffering, kindness, goodness, faithfulness, gentleness, and self-control. All right now, it's all coming together because each of the added ingredients is beginning to complement the others.

When we encounter challenges in life, God tells us to be of good cheer because He has already overcome them. Challenges are good. They show you what you are made of. Challenges help you to grow from one level of faith to another. As much as I love my sister's gumbo, it's really nothing more than just a bunch of juice until she adds the shrimp, the chicken, the crab, and the sausage. Yes, the roux is the foundation that holds it all together. However, the combination of the ingredients on the inside coupled with the heat is what produces the real flavor. God knows what you need in order to grow and mature in Him. Every ingredient has a specific purpose, but when they all come together and are carefully placed at just the right temperature for just the right amount of time, the final outcome will always be perfect.

Don't be afraid to go through the heated places, I guarantee you they will indeed bring out your real flavor. Oh, how I thank God for a gumbo life!

In the Solitude of My Sanctuary
(St. Luke 5:16)

Have you ever felt the need to just cry? I know I have. The last few years of my life, I have truly come to appreciate the power of my tears. They help me to release. They help me to replenish myself. They help me to reboot spiritually, mentally, and emotionally. After emerging from a good cry, I feel revived. I feel a resurgence of strength. I used to believe that crying was a sign of weakness, but I thank God that now I know different. When I lost my babies, I cried. When two of my godmothers passed, I cried. When my daddy passed, I cried. When my mama passed, oh my God, I cried. When God speaks to me, sometimes I cry. When I am happy, sometimes I cry. When I am in a place of total peace—you guessed it—sometimes I cry.

There are five bedrooms in my home, but there is one in particular that has such a special anointing. It is upstairs facing east. Biblically speaking, the eastward direction has great meaning. I call it my "Green Room." It holds so much peace. A beautiful lime-green, red, and white floral comforter adorns the bed with lots of plush and fluffy pillows. The windows are accented by lime-green sheers that provide a certain garden-fresh feel to the room when the sun shines through them. Every morning when I rise, I go to this room and open the blinds to allow the sunshine in. If there is an undercurrent of something in my spirit, I can go and just quietly sit in this room and listen as my worship music plays softly. I wait for the peace of God to overtake me. The elders used to call it "stilling away" simply because you are getting away from everybody just to get still before the Lord. I love the private intimacy that He and I share. A few minutes pass as I am still. A few more minutes pass as I listen. Then finally, there's a breakthrough in my spirit … *ahhhh!*

The tears begin to fall, and the Lord begins to reveal what's really going on deep within me. This is such a refreshing experience.

Where do you go when you need to have a good cry? Do you have a designated sanctuary? Do you have a place where you can go and know without a doubt that God will meet you there? We all need one. Being a pastor's wife, I have heard many messages preached by my husband. However, there was one in particular that he preached at the Greater Galilee Church in which the Holy Spirit used him in such an unusually powerful and phenomenal way to usher in an overwhelming spirit of peace into the atmosphere. A shift took place in the sanctuary on that day that was just intoxicating! It was as though burdens were simply floating out of the hearts of the saints and into the heavens. Men and women alike were crying out to God. Hands were lifted. There was such a sweet spirit that filled the sanctuary. As I looked around with tears in my own eyes, I was so humbled by what God was allowing me to see in the spirit. No feeling comes close to being in the presence of the Holy Spirit. There is absolutely nothing like it. For me, it is a peace that lovingly covers me like a warm blanket fresh out of the dryer. Or better yet, it's like walking outside on a spring day with no umbrella as a fresh rain is falling from the heavens.

I just love being in the presence of the Lord! In His presence, there really is fullness of joy. Being in His presence is mystical, magical, and majestic. It's a feeling you never want to end. If you don't already have one, I encourage you to prayerfully find your sanctuary. Create that special place just for you and the Lord to meet daily. At home, no one ever goes into my Green Room. When my heart is heavy, I can just enter in and allow myself to surrender and become totally free. Whenever I begin to feel like life is about to take me under, I simply escape to the solitude of my safe place and into the presence of the Lord. He's always there waiting for me to arrive. Although I enter in one way, I exit quite differently. I exit with a greater sense of peace, purpose, and power, all because I have spent time with my Father in the solitude of my sanctuary.

Is There a Judas at Your Table?
(Matthew 26–28)

I hail from a long line of awesome cooks. In my family, the girls were taught at a very young age to prepare a balanced meal. Of course, cooking was only one of thousands of lessons my mother taught my sister and me. As diligent as my mother was about training my sister and me to become strong women, there were some things that my mother did that just totally confused me— that is, until I myself became a woman and grew in wisdom and spiritual understanding. As children growing up, everybody ate from my parents' table. My parents' home was always filled with people who enjoyed their culinary gifts. The confusing thing was, they fed and helped those they knew liked them as well as those they *knew* didn't. One incident in particular comes to mind. My mother was helping to feed and provide for a woman who had fallen on hard times only to have her begin saying very ugly and negative things about my mother and eventually stop speaking to her altogether when she got on her feet. One day, I overheard my mother crying to my father about this situation, and of course, I wanted to handle this woman myself because she hurt my mama. Now, if you had the same kind of upbringing I had, you knew not to mess with anybody's mama!

Well, that was many years ago. My parents are resting peacefully with the Lord, and my sister and I are now both mature women with families of our own, teaching our children many of the same lessons, including feeding and helping anyone in need. When we would bring things to Mama's attention about the events of the past, she would simply say, "Don't ever worry about what people do to you or say about you because God will handle them." And boy was she right! A very dear lady who now sleeps with the Lord by the name of Pearline Hampton once told me at the age of fifteen to always pray for discernment. When I would ask her what discernment was, she would simply say in her aged and deep, raspy voice, "It's spiritual sense, baby! Many folk got common sense, but they ain't got a lick of spiritual sense!" She was so funny but always straight to the point. As I grow in the Lord, I have come to realize that there will always be a Judas at the table in some form or another. However, reacting to these people is futile because God knew it first! God protects His children, and when you are covered by Him, no devil dead or alive can destroy you!

When you read today's passage of scriptures, you will discover that Jesus knew Judas would betray Him. It was actually part of the divine plan, yet Jesus invited him to dinner anyway. It was Judas who was in the dark about what was really going on, not Jesus! In fact, Judas was a very critical piece of the puzzle because it would be his deadly and deceptive kiss that would ultimately lead to Jesus's death, burial, and resurrection!

Moral of the story, never lose your cool over the presence of a Judas, because his or her presence, when handled properly, only leads to your "greater"! This person's actions may knock you down for a minute, but I assure you, if you follow God's lead, you *will* rise again. So go ahead and invite Judas to the table; after all, he needs to eat too.

Is Your Spirit Man on Life Support?

(Romans 10:17)

Life support is the intervention used by medical professionals to sustain a person's life for a period of time. A person who is in need of life support in most cases has suffered a serious traumatic injury that has led to vital organ failures, thus rendering him or her unable to survive on his or her own. Life support is a necessary tool used as a means of providing temporary support until the person is able to begin breathing on his or her own again. In most cases, a person who requires life support is indeed unconscious, in a comatose state, completely oblivious of what's going on around him or her.

My father, prior to his passing in August 2012, suffered a stroke that left him powerless to walk or to talk. As he lay in the hospital for months, between my mother, my siblings, and me, there was someone with him at all times. The doctors would encourage us to talk to him, read to him, let him listen to music and so forth for the purpose of creating some degree of normalcy. My sister and I would wash his face, brush and oil his hair, lotion his skin, and put cologne on him to prepare him for the many guests he received. Regardless of the fact that he was on life support, he was still *Daddy* to us! My father's condition was a physical one. However, believe it or not, there are many who suffer the same type of condition but in a spiritual sense, which brings me to my question for you …

Is your spirit man on life support? Is he unconscious? Is he oblivious to what's going on around him? Has he suffered a traumatic injury to the point of his heart shutting down by common conditions, such as bitterness, hard-heartedness, unforgiveness, envy, anger, jealousy, and so on? The fact is many Christians do not realize the power they have. It has been said—and it is true—that ignorance can be very expensive. Many times when faced with a crisis or dilemma, the first thing most Christians do is spiral into a state of anxiety. Why is that, when God says to be anxious for nothing? Because anxiety is what comes naturally, and that's the problem.

As believers, we are never to become guilty of doing what comes naturally but instead should do what comes spiritually. Romans 10:17 confirms that faith cometh by hearing and hearing by the word of God. We as believers need to position ourselves to hear a word from the Lord. Your faith is strengthened through the word of God and consistent fellowship with other believers. What are you listening to? Or better yet, whom are you listening to? Whose mouth is your ear constantly connected to? Are these people's words pumping life into you or draining it out of you? These are some very critical questions each of us must ask ourselves in order to move into the position of living a truly blessed life. It has been said—and it is true—that whatever you hear the most is what you will develop an appetite for. As sad as it is, many Christians are nothing more than the walking dead. The Lord just has not pulled the plug yet. It is our responsibility as believers to make the conscious decision to position ourselves to hear a word from the Lord. The word of God is the necessary ingredient needed to pump life back into your spirit man. Proverbs 18:21 reminds us that death and life are in the power of the tongue! So what are you speaking out of your mouth? I guarantee that if you check your words, you will find the source of the problem! Proverbs 4:23 reminds us to be careful how we think because our lives are shaped by our thoughts. Hmmm ... how is that connected here? I'll tell you. The connection is this: what you think becomes what you say, what you say becomes what you do, what you do becomes who you are, who you are will determine the life you will live. Got it?

If your spirit man is on life support, allow him a visit from the Father. Allow the Holy Spirit to come in and minister to him. Allow the Holy Spirit to come in and touch him. God loves you so much that He has made available to you just the right dose of spiritually intravenous medicine needed in order to pump life back into your spirit man so that he can begin to live again. The prescription was written over two thousand years ago, but the decision is yours to connect to the divine drip.

I've Fallen, and I Can't Get Up
(Galatians 6:1)

Have you ever been in the company of someone who was negatively speaking about another person who happens to be going through a difficult season? Maybe the situation was brought on by a bad decision, trusting the wrong person or just plain ole rebellion. However, regardless of the details that landed him or her in his or her current predicament, the fact is this person is in it. All of us have been on both ends of this spectrum—as the victim and the perpetrator. However, we must remember that everybody at some point in life has fallen into sin and has needed the assistance of a more spiritually mature brother or sister. The apostle Paul teaches us in Galatians 6:1 that if someone falls as a result of sin, then it is our place as the more spiritual believer to lovingly forgive and help restore him or her. Throughout the period of restoration, it is very important to keep our comments to ourselves as well as remain confidential. Reason being, one day we may find ourselves needing forgiveness and restoration for the very same thing. It is the more mature believer who knows that we should be very careful about what we sow, knowing that what we sow will be the very thing that we reap.

In life, everybody struggles with something. Now my struggle may not be the same as yours, but the fact is we all struggle at some point. No person is exempt. Alcohol, crack cocaine, heroin, prescription drugs, nicotine, sex, food, shopping, the Internet, gambling, pornography ... the list is endless. But let's clarify something regarding addiction. An addiction is nothing more than a habit, obsession, craving, or infatuation with something (or somebody). What we must remember is just as sin is sin, the same goes for addiction, and they both have the power to destroy everything and everybody in their path! If you are not struggling with an addiction, then it is only by the amazing grace of God. Life has a way of fooling us into thinking that we are superior to others because we are not standing on a street corner with a sign or somewhere selling our bodies for another *hit*. The only difference between them and us is a simple decision.

God has not commanded us to become judges and jurors regarding other people's situations, but He has commanded us to help restore them. Many families have been mangled by the perfect storm of addiction and deceit because the two have the power to leave relationships in shambles. Addiction destroys trust. Addiction violates. Family members are worn down physically, mentally, emotionally, and sometimes even financially because of mounting lies and deceit. Believe it or not, we communicate with people every day who are quietly struggling with an addiction of some sort and some are even up close and personal to us. We sit right beside people in church on Sundays who struggle with a secret addiction. Yes, that's right. Even in the Lord's house from the pulpit to the pews, people are struggling with addictions. But just as God patiently looks beyond all our faults and meets our needs, we must exercise the same degree of unconditional love and patience for others. I don't dare pen these words without experience. As they say, "Been there, done that."

Love never fails, according to 1 Corinthians 13. Love is patient. Love is kind. We are quick to tell people to trust God, but the point we are missing is, as believers, we are responsible for extending the hand of God. As children, one of the first lessons we were taught was the Golden Rule: "Do unto others as you would have them do unto you" (Luke 6:31 KJV). Having said that, I will leave this thought with you, "If I were in their shoes, I would ..."

Just Bloom!
(Romans 8:31)

I have suffered much pain and heartache in my life. Some of it was self-inflicted, some orchestrated by the enemy, and, yes, some God-ordained, designed to take me to the next level. However, regardless of the nature of pain's origin, it has always worked together for my good (Romans 8:28 KJV). Pain is an indicator. It clearly dictates to you when something is wrong. It lets you know that something is out of order. Pain is one of the greatest teachers in the world, for its lessons will never be forgotten.

In His Sermon on the Mount (Matthew 5–7), Jesus taught the people many valuable lessons. His lesson plans included anger, revenge, divorce, vows, love for enemies, giving, prayer and fasting, money and possessions, judging, and the list goes on. Each of these very critical lessons is designed to help us live victorious lives, regardless of the conditions surrounding us.

Some time ago, while outside on my patio, I was sitting and enjoying the rain. I absolutely love the sound, smell, and calming effects of rain. While I was sitting there, relaxed in the moment, God showed me something that provided me with a high that could rival the best drug on the black market. He had me to look down at the crowd of flowerpots that I had out on the patio to be thrown away. Each of them was full of dirt. Not only that, but the dirt had become hardened as a result of the surrounding elements. They were full of weeds sprouting everywhere in their attempt to take over my patio. They were ugly to look at, full of clutter and old dirt. But then there was one little pot in the crowd. There was something so very special about this particular pot. This one little pot in the crowd had holes in the bottom of it on all four sides. And although it suffered the same effects as all the other pots of dirt, *this baby was different!* When I got up out of my chair to inspect the pot more closely, I realized that there were lush, green sprouts that had grown through the holes in the bottom of it. Jesussssss! My soul got happy! I felt a God kind of rush go all through me. The excitement was overwhelming as tears filled my eyes.

Saints, when situations of life try to cause you to become hard-hearted, if you are truly a child of God, you have been especially equipped with all the right stuff to bloom. When people dig ditches for you, using the shovels of guilt and shame ... bloom. When they try to bury you with your past ... bloom. When people lie on you ... bloom. When they persecute you ... bloom. When they constantly remind you of your sordid past ... bloom. When they question the God in you ... bloom. When they bring up your past mistakes ... bloom. When you are not their choice for the promotion and they plot against you receiving the promotion and the money ... bloom!

One thing I have come to know is this. There is never a need to respond to the comments of others. Why? Simply because for those who really matter, a response is not necessary and for those who don't, a response will never suffice. Not only that, but if God be for you ... He is greater than the whole world against you, so all you simply need to do is *bloom*!

Life Really Is a Choice
(Proverbs 4:23–27)

Are you pleased with where your life is right now? If not, why not speak change into existence? As believers, the word of God teaches us that our words have much power. Just as the farmer who moves about the land, dropping seeds into the soil of the earth in hopes that it will produce a bountiful harvest, we too must realize that our words are the seeds that we drop daily, and they too will produce a harvest. I tell people all the time, "What I say is what I sow!" meaning that each and every time I allow a word, positive or negative, to fall from my lips, I set things in motion, thus shaping the world around me.

Proverbs 6:2 reminds us that we are snared by the words of our mouths. A snare is a trap. In other words, once you speak a thing, the atmosphere begins to rearrange itself to honor what you say, whether good or bad, again shaping the world around you. Many of us have been tricked by the enemy into giving our power away. We have allowed our inner selves to become contaminated by our outer circumstances, and this is totally out of order. If you are a Bible reader, you know that in the beginning, God gave dominion and power to humans, according to Genesis 1:22. However, because of sin, we now walk in spiritual blindness, not living the life God fully intended for us to live. This is in essence why we experience great struggles with the simple things of life. We have spoken so many things out of our mouths that don't line up with the word of God until now our inner selves are totally confused and spiritually impotent.

How do we get back on track? How do we reverse the curse of impotence and get back to producing the life God originally intended for us to have? Well, first you pray and ask God's forgiveness for the careless words you have spoken. Then, as you move forward in the spirit of repentance, you begin speaking and believing the word. Time is a precious commodity, so don't waste it beating up on yourself; after all, who knows the story better than you, so no need to nurse it or rehearse it. Instead, move forward with your head and your heart on the same page, believing God's word. Know that you are an overcomer simply because you are a part of a chosen generation, a royal priesthood and a holy nation of God (1 Peter 2:9). Know that because you were created in His image and fashioned for His glory that you are victorious. You must know that because death and life are in the power of your tongue (Proverbs 18:21), you are a power shifter in the earth. It's not hard at all. It is, however, about knowing and believing the right stuff all the time because what's in you will come out of you.

I encourage you to allow the word of God to help you release the negative and receive the positive. I invite you to think only on those things that are true, honest, pure, lovely, and of a good report (Philippians 4:8), for it still holds true that where the mind goes, the person is sure to follow.

Lord, I Thank You ...

(Psalm 28:7)

In my personal opinion, there are no words in the English language that can describe the black church experience. In the black church, you find rich, meaningful hymns. There you can enjoy fervent spirit-filled fellowship, coupled with the intense feeling of family. The experience in general is one that truly ministers to the soul. The lyrics of the old-school hymns and melodies tell the story of a profound journey. Sometimes when I am alone, a song will enter into my spirit and I just can't seem to contain myself. The tears begin to flow uncontrollably. But they are not tears of sadness. In fact, they are tears that spring from the river of joy that flows deep within me. Has this ever happened to you? Have you ever encountered such a sweet experience, just you and the Lord? Oh my goodness, the feeling is indescribable! So many people are of the belief that you need a choir, praise team, or preacher in order to tap into the vein of true worship. But I beg to differ.

There is one song that I absolutely love to hear, and that is "Lord, I Thank You," sung by Pastor E. Dewey Smith of the Greater Travelers Rest Church in Decatur, Georgia. Sometimes late at night, as I am preparing to write, I go to YouTube and listen to this song over and over. Oh, how it ministers to my spirit. When I think about every mountain that the Lord has brought me over and every valley He has seen me through, before I know it, my hands go up, the tears come down, and I am in an all-out praise party all by myself!

I owe God my life! It was in June of 1985, at the age of seventeen, that I received my very first prophetic word from my late pastor, Hayward Edward Joseph Wiggins. What a phenomenal servant of God this man was! After hearing this word, I walked in rebellion for many years (twenty-three to be exact) simply because I did not want the responsibility of the life the Lord had revealed to me that I was predestined to live. Even now as I think about it, I am so very grateful that God spared my life during those years. I can talk to you about it because I lived it. Many times, I rebelled against God because I just hoped that He would somehow change His mind about what He wanted my purpose to be and just let me off the hook. It is so amazing how you can be so focused on running away from something that you don't even realize that the very thing you are running from is what you are running right into all at the same time.

Many years have passed since that great Sunday morning in June, and I am so humbled and honored that God was patient with me. Because He loved me, He equipped me to withstand the very painful purification process that He had for me. He loved me through my foolishness. He forgave me of my foolishness. He chastised me for my foolishness. But He did it all in love. I have been through the fire many times but never burned. Just like with the Hebrew boys, He showed up in the fire with me and saved me, and He will do the same for you. I have been through many storms, and just like for the children of Israel, He always provided me with a way of escape. He will do the same for you. God, in His infinite wisdom, knew precisely what it would take to bring me to this place in ministry alongside my husband, who also happens to be an awesome servant leader. He knew exactly what brick-wall experiences I needed to press deeper into Him in order to one day be prepared to encourage you in the spirit of transparency. He knew just what I needed for such a time as this. I am equally grateful for parents who were patient with me, prayed for me, and never gave up on me. I am thankful to God for allowing them to live to see the prophetic word come to pass in my life. One thing I have learned is that every spiritual dot in life is connected to another one. Once all the dots have been connected, you end up with a beautiful and priceless masterpiece. It's a story that can be told only by you.

As a child of God, always remember that whatever is over your head is always under His feet. Be patient with yourself as you follow Him. Be patient with your children as they mature in Him. By all means, be patient with others who may not know Him. One of the worst things we can do as believers is cause other believers to stumble. Therefore, allow the light of the Lord to shine in you, over you, and through you. I promise when you least expect it, you will discover that your light was just enough light for the dark path that someone else was on. Remember the Lord smiles on those He is pleased with.

My Eyes Are Open, but I Can't See a Thing
(1 Peter 5:7)

Several years ago, my husband and I had to take our daughter back and forth to an eye specialist because she had been complaining about not being able to "see clearly." Each visit consisted of one test after another, only to keep coming up with the same results and no real explanation. Finally, the doctor said to me, "Mom, I am going to have to run some more extensive tests because I do not understand why I cannot correct her vision." In complete agreement and out of concern for our daughter's optical health, I immediately gave the doctor clearance to do what needed to be done. Before the visit ended, I met with the doctor one-on-one, and she said to me, "I am really concerned about this because I have never seen such a situation. Based on the results of the routine tests, she should be seeing clearly. Therefore, I am going to order some more extensive tests that will examine her brain in the areas behind her eyes to see what's really going on." Immediately, I became a little anxious about it all but was quickly reminded that giving in to anxiety was not an option. Therefore, I began to pray silently and make my requests known to the Lord.

Has there ever been a time when you felt as though your focus was off? Not to worry—this happens to everybody. Sometimes the magnitude of the challenges we face can cause us to lose our focus because we set our sights on the problem and not the problem solver. God never intended for us to handle our problems alone, which is why He instructs us in 1 Peter 5:7 to cast our cares on Him. Because of our limited abilities, it is imperative that we immediately place our problems in the Master's hands. God is sovereign. Therefore, He reserves the right to go behind the scenes and examine us more closely for the purpose of seeing what's really going on. My daughter's eye situation is physical, but so many times our inability to see clearly is spiritual. All of us have been guilty of allowing people and situations to interfere with our focus. In Psalm 138:8, God provides us with a sweet reminder that He will perfect those things that concern us. So if your lack of focus is a concern to you, it is a concern to God. It is never God's desire to see His children stressed out by life. When you search the scriptures, you will discover that He has given us dominion over all the earth (Genesis 1:26). He has given us the ability to call things into existence. He has made us overcomers. He has given us His word, and there is power in His word! With that kind of power, why be stressed?

If we are to be victorious over the enemy, we must begin speaking the word of God out of our mouths with bold faith. God's promises are endless. Don't allow the enemy to rob you of your focus any longer. If you are not there yet, confess it to God and allow the Holy Spirit to minister to you. He's got you, but you have to know that for yourself. Everything you need, God has it. All you have to do is seek Him, and you are sure to find what you need. Opening your eyes is not enough; you must also open your heart.

Never Judge a Book
(Matthew 7:1–3)

Many people have made the huge mistake of judging someone they don't know based on the opinions of others. This is not only dangerous; it is unfair and very spiritually immature. When you construct an opinion of someone you don't even know according to what someone else thinks or says about that person, you are in many ways relinquishing all opportunities for a divine connection. In the words of my pastor, "Pull out your calculator, and help me figure this one out." Why is it that we judge people any kind of way but when people judge us, we get angry and feel mistreated? That's crazy! If we feel as though we have the right to be who we are, then why do we attempt to place restrictions on somebody else? Why do we feel the need to try to police others into being who and what we want them to be? Our featured scripture today deals with this very subject. Matthew 7:1–3 firmly instructs us as believers not to judge other people if we ourselves don't want to be judged. That's crystal clear, and it leaves no room for questions. It goes on to further advise us that whatever measure we use to judge someone else, the exact same measure will be used to judge us, and this is always where things get tricky.

The sad reality is this: the reason why we try to police others into being what we feel they should be is rooted in our own selfishness and insecurities. Nevertheless, we must practice playing fair with people at all times. God is about diversity. He created each of us differently and equipped each of us with a unique set of gifts and talents. But different doesn't mean better; it simply means different. Do you know how boring and uneventful the world would be if we were all created just alike with the same thoughts, actions, and beliefs? Just the thought of that is scary. We are all created in His image and after His likeness, according to Genesis 1:25–27. Therefore, we have been uniquely designed to give Him glory through the use of the gifts and talents placed within us. Diversity strengthens. Discord weakens. Whenever we seek to undermine and disrespect the uniqueness of others, we not only rob them, but we rob ourselves and the entire body of Christ. If we learn to embrace what others bring to the table, the entire body of Christ will be made stronger. However, this constant bickering back and forth over the smallest issues (especially in the church) becomes a stumbling block for the whole world. I have judged, and I have been judged, and honestly, neither scenario was profitable.

Want to know how to become more secure with yourself? Allow yourself to become vulnerable by facing the giants of your past. People ask me all the time, "How can you be so open about your experiences?" and I simply tell them that I am no different from anybody else. Every person has been through something and is going through something, but I just simply choose not to be a prisoner of my own past. I share my life with others to strengthen them by letting them know that someone has been down the road that they are now traveling and is willing to help guide them out of the darkness. The world would be a much better place if we all really did live by the Golden Rule. Nobody is perfect but the Master Himself, but all of us should be striving for perfection. What if we all tried to genuinely love and accept one another? What if we were truly authentic in our behaviors toward one another? What if we operated in honesty and integrity with one another at all times? What if we passed on the corrupt communication and allowed our words to be seasoned with grace (Colossians 4:6)? I could go on, but I am certain you understand my point.

In the words of the late great Michael Jackson, "If you want to make the world a better place, take a look at yourself and make a change." Besides, after all is said and done, it is not your job to like me; it's mine.

Obeying the Voice
(Deuteronomy 28)

How diligent are you when it comes to obeying the voice of God? Are you obedient, but only on your own terms? Do you carry out the instruction, but with a hint of attitude? How many times have you heard someone say that they compromised in order to keep the peace? I am sure we all have heard this statement before. I must warn you that when it comes to obeying the voice of God, there is no room for compromise. Obeying the voice of God is keeping the peace. Before I go any further, let me inform you that delayed obedience is disobedience.

In Deuteronomy 28, God deals quite candidly with the children of Israel regarding the blessings of obedience and the curses of disobedience. When we are given a specific instruction by Him, we are to carry it out exactly as we are instructed with diligence. To ponder our opinion or talk it over with friends is a dangerous thing to do. The results can be catastrophic, to say the very least. The word of God promises to set us high above all nations of the earth when we diligently hearken unto the voice of the Lord. While this may sound good, I need to advise you of the flip side of things. In verse 15 of Deuteronomy 28, God says, "If we choose not to obediently heed His voice and observe to do all of His commandments, curses will come." Any believer in his or her right mind wants to be blessed by God. I must admit, I don't know of a single believer who is just hungering and thirsting for God to curse him or her. But as with all things, the choice is clearly yours.

Here is one major problem. Too many times, we allow the voices of others to take precedence over the voice of God. We allow people's limited, logical, and educated opinions to cause us to become disobedient and miss out on our blessings. God says what He means and He means what He says.

To be diligent about something means to persist at it or to press forward into doing something with a certain degree of carefulness. This is what God requires from each of His children. For those of us who are parents, we should understand this principle better than anybody. When we instruct our children to do something, how irritated do we become when they exhibit a lazy or ungrateful attitude when carrying out the instruction? Or better yet, how do we feel when they have done it but in their own way or on their own terms? Not happy at all, right? This tactic of the enemy leaves us as parents feeling disrespected, used, and angry.

Let's trade places with God for just a moment. How would you feel if you constantly provided for people, protected them, forgave them, granted them new mercies, prayed for them, loved them unconditionally, healed them, restored them, and responded to their every cry only to have them second-guess your instructions with an ungrateful attitude? Every one of us at some point has exhibited this type of behavior, but God's grace is sufficient, according to 2 Corinthians 12:9. Therefore, when we discover the error of our ways, it is then that we must immediately go before the throne of grace in the spirit of repentance and humbly for ask forgiveness for our disobedience. Afterward, not only will we feel totally refreshed, renewed, and revived through the power of the Holy Spirit, but we will also regain peace in our soul. Obeying the voice of God not only promotes spiritual peace but also creates a deeper level of intimacy with the Father.

Open for Renovations
(Matthew 5:14–16)

Several years ago, I was returning from lunch at the Crowne Plaza Hotel in Downtown Houston with some coworkers. We walked past a building that was being renovated, and the sign out front said, "Closed for Renovations." This sign lingered in my thoughts, and I did not know why until the Lord woke me up early the next morning to tell me why. He explained to me that although the world's way of doing things is to shut everything down when a building is under construction, it is just the opposite for the children of God. As believers, our signs should always say to the world, "Open, Renovations Taking Place."

As I leaped out of bed and got to my computer, the Holy Spirit took me straight to Matthew 5:14–16. Because we are the light of the world, people should be able to see and experience the divine reconstructive work that is taking place in our lives. People should witness the divine stripping away of old thoughts and habits being replaced by new ones; the tearing down of walls that have been erected over time by anger, bitterness, unforgiveness, insecurity, rebellion, bad attitudes, miscommunication, and so on; the divine hammering and chiseling away at doubt and self-pity that takes up residence in our minds. I think you now get the picture.

The very next time you see a building that is closed for renovations, I encourage you to stop and offer up praise to God for being "Open for Renovations," because believe it or not, somebody somewhere is always watching you! So what does your sign say to the world? Remember when the believer keeps the word, the word will keep the believer!

Operating with a Purpose
(Romans 8:28)

I love to read, and one of my most treasured books is *You're Born an Original, Don't Die a Copy!* This book, written by John L. Mason, speaks directly to the soul of the reader with precision and clarity. Derived from the scriptures, it is inundated with short anecdotes, encouraging the reader to seek out his or her divine purpose in life and walk in it. What would you do if you witnessed a cat barking or a dog meowing or even a cow clucking? If you are anything like me, you would wonder what in the world was going on. Well, how many of God's most treasured creations are walking around trying to be like somebody else? We see it every day. People make others a case study, trying to become more like them because they think more highly of others than they do themselves. Did you know that trying to operate according to somebody else's purpose will profit you nothing? God has an intended plan and purpose for each of us, and the only way we can totally be fulfilled in this life is to find out what it is and walk it out. In addition, what we are actually saying to God is "You made a mistake when You created me!" Oh, how dare the clay say such a thing to the potter? Saints, God divinely created each and every one of us with something special that the world needs and only we can provide. But how can we expect things to work together for our good when we choose to operate according to somebody else's purpose? When we do this, we in essence rob others and the world in general of our special gift.

Let's go deeper. Why are we so quick to want somebody else's life or gift instead of our own? Two of the main reasons are fear and insecurity. Many people fear they are not good enough. Countless others are insecure because they constantly feed on the fear that they are not good enough or will fail. What makes a person insecure is believing the lies and tricks of the enemy. However, when you walk in your intended purpose and operate in your God-ordained gift, that makes you enough.

I strongly encourage you to take some personal time and examine those areas that you have struggled with. Ask yourself some tough questions and then get a piece of paper and write down what comes to mind. You will discover you have known the answers all along. However, maybe you chose to ignore them or you just simply did not know how to handle them. If it's the latter, here's my response to you: the word works. The Lord says, "So shall my word be that goeth forth out of my mouth: it shall not return unto me void, but it shall accomplish that which I please, and it shall prosper in the thing whereto I sent it" (Isaiah 55:11 KJV). There you have it, straight from the mouth of the Master. God has predestined a specific purpose for your life, and when you receive it and walk in it, you will be amazed at how all things really will work together for your good not only because you love God but because you have obediently chosen to walk according to His purpose for you. When this happens, great and mighty things are destined to follow. Be encouraged as you walk in your divine purpose.

Plastic Plantation
(*Proverbs 22:7*)

All year long, stores are inundated with people pushing plastic for the sole purpose of perpetrating perfection! Here's what I mean. In the free world, many people are still very caught up with the persona of looking like they have risen to a certain status level, thinking that this will cause them to become the envy of other people. Yes, many are still guilty of buying things they don't need with money they don't have, trying to impress people they don't even know or like. Others are guilty of trying to financially jog with the Jordans when they can't even walk with the Wilsons. It is truly sad that so many are willing to trade their financial future for a mere puffed-up borrowed image of what they think is success.

The Bible teaches us in Proverbs 22:7 that the rich rule over the poor and the borrower is slave to the lender ... a.k.a. a *plastic plantation*. It's never our needs that cause us financial heartache; instead, it's our wants. Our wants consist of those things that we crave and buy to feed our flesh. They feed our never-ending addiction to satisfying our hidden insecurities and inadequacies. To constantly feed the flesh is the equivalent of feeding a slot machine that will never pay off. Why? Because the flesh is about instant gratification, and it is always hungry for more, more, more. Then just like that, we wake up one day only to discover that we are thousands of dollars in debt with absolutely nothing to show for it. With mounting debt come stress, anxiety, sickness, depression, and sometimes even death.

The book of Proverbs notes that there are many things that are better than money in the bank, such as wisdom, insight, a good reputation, and a gracious spirit to name a few. Yes, I can hear you thinking, *Yeah, but it's money that makes the world go 'round,* and maybe so, but in what direction?

When you consistently exhibit these attributes that the Bible names, money will come. However, it is quite a tragedy to purchase the finest crib, cars, and clothes (all on credit of course) just to provide yourself with a small degree of temporary satisfaction. In essence, this makes you nothing more than an exquisitely wrapped package with nothing inside! Ecclesiastes 7:12 of the Message Bible states, "Wisdom is better when it's paired with money, especially if you get both while you are still living." It also guarantees you double protection when you have wisdom and wealth. In the words of Dr. Clyde McCray, "Having money is not a problem ... but money having you is a huge problem." After all, Matthew 6:24 boldly states that we can't worship both God and money. We must choose. So what will it be, the wise lender or the broke borrower? Just something to think about ...

Pruned for Production
(John 15:1–7)

Many years ago, a metal box fell and cut the top of my foot. While the pain was excruciating, the amount of free-flowing blood was just unbelievable, thus causing me to quickly head straight for the emergency room. By the time I made it to the emergency room, the blood had completely soaked through the bandaging I had wrapped around my foot. As I entered, the emergency room nurses were shocked by the enormous amount of blood I had lost only to discover that the size of the cut producing this kind of blood loss just did not match. The ER doctor then commented that it is not the size of a cut that matters but instead the depth of it. The cut was only about an inch long, but the depth of it was almost three layers. Of course I had to get a tetanus shot because it was a metal box, and getting the tetanus shot would protect me against any future infections just in case there were any metal fragments left in my body. After the doctor had cleaned out the cut and flushed it for any potential leftover fragments, the time had come to stitch it up. The stitching process was a bit lengthy, simply because the doctor had to stitch from the inside out, so to speak. I was then given a prescription for pain and instructed to follow up with my primary care physician.

As time passed, I discovered that the pain was still pretty bad and that my entire foot began to take on a different look. It was hot, red, and swollen. Because of fear, I decided to rush in to see my doctor only to discover that my foot had become completely infected. My doctor immediately requested an x-ray. The x-ray revealed that something was indeed still left on the inside of my foot. As a result, I had to be recut, reflushed, and restitched all because of a tiny metal fragment that remained on the inside, which affected my ability to heal on the outside.

Did you know that leftover residue on the inside can affect your ability to heal on the outside? Well, it's true. All of us at some point in life have encountered emotional hurt that cuts pretty deep. Such emotional hurt can sometimes leave us with an infected spirit. But thank God for Jesus because He has the answer for this. Many times, we don't heal because we have chosen not to forgive the guilty party who hurt us. Our refusal to forgive can create an infectious residue that has the ability to severely cripple our spirit man. Saints, sometimes God will allow situations and experiences in our lives as a means of purging certain behaviors and attitudes out of us. To *purge* simply means to remove the undesirable. All of us have some undesirables resting deep within us that are affecting our ability to grow closer to the Lord and produce fruit. Our background scripture clearly explains how and why we must be purged on a regular basis. Purging is a painful process. However, when it is complete, the sound of production can be heard looming over the horizon of our hearts once again.

The Lord, in His infinite wisdom and His unfailing love for us, knows exactly when and how to purge each of His children in an effort to jump-start us to producing fruit again. He purges us because He loves us and knows what is on the inside of us. After He is done cutting us, He then lovingly cleans us up through His word and sends us on our way. Once the entire process is complete and we have been freed of the crippling contaminants, we are again in a position to ask Him for anything according to His will and it shall be done.

Has your fruit production been stalled? If the answer is yes, maybe it's time to head to the divine emergency room for a comprehensive x-ray, as ordered by the Great Physician. You may have to be cut, flushed, and even stitched, but once the process is complete, production will begin again! Don't lose hope, saints. Just like my foot, you may have a scar left, but it remains only as a reminder of the experience you have endured. However, the blessing is the pain is no longer a hindrance and the infection is now gone. Thank God for the divine purging process.

Putting It on Pause
(Matthew 15:11 and 18)

My Saturdays are generally pretty busy. However, if what I am doing is not completed by eight in the evening, it is put on pause while I stop to watch *Welcome to Sweetie Pie's*. *Welcome to Sweetie Pie's* is by far one of my favorite shows on the OWN network channel. I love watching Ms. Robbie handle Tim, Janae, Charles, and the rest of the gang on the show. I am always fascinated by the black family on the big screen. In essence, I get an opportunity to watch different facets of my own life and family in one form or another. The black family experience is a beautiful one—not always pretty but beautiful nonetheless. When we don't see eye to eye on things, our disagreements can sometimes get pretty ugly. I am certain this does exist within other races. However, because I have never been anything other than African American, I can only truthfully speak about us. We love just as hard as we fight, and in the end, we remain family. Sometimes we tend to say hurtful things to one another out of anger, but in the end, we remain family. Movies and shows, such as *Soul Food*, *Good Times*, and *The Cosby Show*, all tell such wonderful stories about the black family experience. Each of these shows pretty truthfully depicts how we handle issues, such as faith in God, love for one another, the pain of tragedy, and overcoming challenges, and in the end, still remain a family solid in our loyalty to one another.

In one of the final episodes of *Welcome to Sweetie Pie's*, the cast members were given the opportunity to watch themselves on the big screen and express their thoughts and feelings about their behavior. Immediately, I thought to myself, *OMG, this is exactly what the Lord will do with us on Judgment Day!* The Bible declares in Matthew 12:35–36 (KJV) that

A good man out of the good treasure of his heart will produce good things, and an evil man out of the evil of his heart will produce evil things. But I say unto you, that every idle word that men shall speak, they shall give account thereof in the Day of Judgment. For by thy words thou shalt be justified, and by thy words thou shalt be condemned.

Wow, that's pretty straightforward. Saints, whatever is going on down on the inside will show up on the outside. Our thoughts give birth to our words, our words give birth to our actions, and our actions give birth to our character and lifestyle. Having said that, when you find your thoughts going astray, just simply put it on pause. When you are about to say something that you know is sure to damage another, put it on pause. Better yet, when you are about to do something that is rude or totally out of line, please put it on pause!

When the Lord calls you before Him and presses the play button on heaven's DVD, will He be pleased with what He sees or hears? Will you, as the featured star, be pleased? If the answer is no, then by all means, put it on pause. The Bible teaches us in Matthew 15:11 that it is not what goes into one's mouth that defiles one but instead what comes out of it, because what comes out of the mouth tells the story of what's in the heart. So the next time you decide to give someone a piece of your mind, put it on pause. The next time somebody gets on your last nerve and you feel the need to tell him or her, put it on pause! Or even still, the next time you decide to throw a rock and hide your hands, please put it on pause!

I encourage you to remember none of us should be deceived because God is not mocked, "for whatsoever a man soweth, that shall he also reap!" (Galatians 6:7). My prayer for you today is that you would receive God's abundant blessings and great favor as you begin exercising your use of the pause button!

Refuse to Be One of the Nine
(Luke 17:11–19)

One of the very first lessons we were taught as children was to say "thank you." My parents believed that teaching us to extend this simple courtesy was not only a sign of gratitude but also a testimony of good home training. One of the most distasteful experiences for me is that of an ungrateful person. Why? Because people don't have to do anything for you, and to have someone extend kindness to you and you not acknowledge it with a simple thank-you is really pushing the envelope. I already know that some of you are feeling me on this one because there are few people who are mature enough to consistently overlook and excuse being taken for granted by other people. We may overlook it the first time and maybe even the second, but any time after that becomes a real issue.

Have you ever been going along, minding your own business, only to have somebody approach you needing help that only you can provide? I believe we have all been there and have extended a helping hand without a second thought. However, the kindness of our hearts quickly takes a turn when someone receives the assistance and just simply walks away without acknowledging it in any way. Well, this is exactly what Jesus experiences in Luke 17. The Bible teaches that while on His way to Jerusalem, He entered a village and was called out by ten men who were lepers. That's right; they called out to Him, asking for mercy. It is profoundly interesting to me that these ten men humbled themselves by referring to Him as "Master" just long enough to get what they needed from Him. Having said that, you do know that not all lepers are dead? My point is that people will appreciate the God in you just long enough to get what they need from you. Jesus, being the master healer that He was, looked at them and gave them specific instructions to go and show themselves to the priests. Here's where things take a turn. As the lepers were on their way to do as instructed, only one of them was paying enough attention to realize that based solely on the word of the Master, he was already healed. As a result, the healed leper who happened to be a Samaritan, immediately turned back to kneel at Jesus's feet and thank Him. This encounter was most intriguing simply because Jesus was a Jew and in those days, the Jews and Samaritans had no dealings with each other. Jews considered themselves as full-blooded and Samaritans as half-breeds. Samaritans were also looked upon as outsiders, so you see, it was actually the outsider who turned back to say thank you. Interesting, huh? Now you have a Jew and a Samaritan in conversation with one another because Jesus does ask the question, "Were not ten healed? Where are the other nine?" Oh, what a tragedy it would be for the Master to heal and deliver us only to have to question our whereabouts because we failed to turn back and say thank you.

Having an ungrateful spirit is very dangerous. When we exhibit this kind of behavior, we are positioning ourselves for self-destruction. Word of advice, when the Master heals or delivers you, don't force Him have to question your whereabouts because you never came back to say thank you. In other words, don't become the miracle that is now missing in action! Instead, immediately turn back, kneel down before the Master, and simply say, "Thank you, sir!"

Releasing the Residue of a Dirty Past

(2 Corinthians 10:5, Romans 8:1–2, 1 John 1:9)

Have you ever done something that you were not proud of? Did it haunt you for a while? Does it still haunt you to this very day? Was it so devastating that it caused you to start viewing life negatively? If you privately answered yes to any of these questions, don't feel alone because everybody who has lived for any length of time has made some bad decisions. When speaking of bad decisions, there are two kinds of people in this world. There are those who choose to release the past, learn from it, and keep it moving, and then there are those who punish themselves by choosing to wallow in their mistakes, causing them to remain stuck in the past. Yes, I clearly said "choose" because it is a choice that you make. As devastating as a bad decision can be, the process of becoming free from it is really not as hard as you may think. The first step is to seek God's forgiveness with a sincere heart, and the second step is to forgive yourself. This second step is always the hardest part of the process for most people simply because they tend to feel that suffering for a while somehow justifies that they knew what they did was wrong. *Newsflash*—You don't need to inflict pain and suffering upon yourself just to confirm that what you did was wrong! In most cases, people enter into a situation already fully knowing that it is wrong, but the flesh ...

Okay, so you have openly and honestly confessed it all to God and asked Him to forgive you ... so now what? How do you really release the residue of a dirty past? You simply stop nursing and rehearsing the past. It is not the mistake itself that is so difficult to deal with; it is the mental and emotional baggage that the mistake produces that can be hard to handle. As humans, we tend to hit the replay button over and over again in our minds, and each time, the effects become more catastrophic to our psyche. This is precisely how the problem grows. In order to stop the growth of anything, you must cease from feeding it, because whatever you feed will grow and whatever you starve will die. Every time thoughts of the past attempt to enter your mind, you have been given some holy help. According to 2 Corinthians 10:5, you have the power to cast down any and all imaginations and every high thing that tries to exalt itself against the knowledge of God in your mind and bring into captivity every thought to the obedience of Christ. If the Lord says you are forgiven, then any thought that enters your mind saying otherwise must be immediately cast down through the confessing of the word. The key is to know your power in the word and speak it with boldness and consistency.

The Message Bible translation of Romans 8:1–2 further reminds us that "with the arrival of Jesus, the Messiah, that fateful dilemma is resolved. Those who enter into Christ's being-here-for-us no longer have to live under a continuous, low-lying black cloud. A new power is in operation. The Spirit of life in Christ, like a strong wind, has magnificently cleared the air, freeing you from a fated lifetime of brutal tyranny at the hands of sin and death." So there you have it, straight from the mouth of the Master.

Remember 1 John 1:9, saints: "If we confess our sins, He is faithful and just to forgive us our sins, and to cleanse us from all unrighteousness" and that includes any and all residue left behind.

Seasons
(Galatians 6:9)

As a child growing up, I was always taught the basic yet critical elements needed to provide me with the solid educational foundation for a successful life—my ABCs, my colors, and how to add, subtract, multiply, and divide numbers. I learned all about the earth and her sister planets. I learned the basics of meteorology, which included what causes rain, thunder, lightning, and so forth. I learned all about farming and agriculture and how the farmer rises early in the morning to go out and plant seeds for the purpose of one day (at the appointed time, of course) being able to reap a harvest from the seeds he or she has planted.

I also learned about seasons. According to humanity's system, there are four seasons—winter, spring, summer, and fall. However, I will stand face-to-face with any educational scholar and argue that a fifth season truly does exist. It is so very intriguing to me how people really believe that we are instrumental in creating anything. In fact, people take credit for God's handiwork all the time. Although many manufacturers exist, people need to understand there is only *one* creator!

It wasn't until I became a serious student of the word of God that I came to know all about a fifth season called "due season." Thank God for this season. The Bible promises us in Galatians 6:9 that we shall reap in *due* season if we faint not. This passage of scripture begins with the Lord's instruction to the believer not to become weary in well-doing. I just love how God knows all, sees all, and hears all. But why did He tell us this? He told us because He knew that we would face great challenges, some that would even cause us to want to give up. However, He provides us with this promise for the sole purpose of helping us continue in the fight, knowing that we will reap many benefits in the end if we don't quit.

Satan is doing his job and doing it well. He is a liar. In fact, he is the father of lies, according to John 8:44. Trust me when I say, I am well aware of the fact that when I am treating others the way I want to be treated, when I am loving my neighbor as myself, when I am going about doing good toward others, when I am living according to the principles of God's word, Satan is not standing across the street in a cheerleader's uniform with pom-poms, jumping up and down, shouting, "Go, Val!" It's just not in his nature. But I will tell you what he is doing. He is roaming around, seeking a way to devour you (1 Peter 5:8). He is looking for ways to steal from you, to kill you, and to destroy you (John 10:10). Don't get offended; it's just what he does because it's who he is.

I thank God that I have learned that when people do something offensive to me, it's not them. Instead, it's the spirit that they have allowed to operate within them. When they lie on you ... treat them well. Yes, even when they dig ditches for you and have the sweat to prove it ... offer them a cool glass of water and continue to treat them well. When they slander your name and attempt to destroy your character and reputation ... pray for them. Is it difficult sometimes to know that people are working to destroy you? Of course it is. Do you sometimes grow weary in well-doing and simply want to give up? Of course you do. However, if you keep your eye on the real prize and remain focused, you will reap the ultimate reward in the end for your labor.

Saints, Satan does his best work in the dark, but the blessing is when God brings you through it (and He will), He will cause His light to shine brightly upon you for everybody to see it!

Secret Service Agents Need Not Apply
(Luke 9:26)

I remember growing up as a child in the Baptist church, how a combination of rich fellowship, good music, and the preached gospel would spark a Holy Ghost party like no other. Every Sunday, the mothers of the church would be dressed in pristine fashion in all their white as they took their rightful place in the pews. However, regardless of how properly dressed they were for Sunday morning worship, they never allowed anything to get in the way of their praise. Out of nowhere, they would break out in a full praise as an expression of gratitude to God for just how good He had been to them. Some would run, others would dance, and yet others would just simply get their war cry on! Whatever the expression, the elders of the church were determined to boldly praise God. The deacons would begin worship with an Old 100, and everybody from the oldest to the youngest knew how to jump right in with the chorus. It was absolutely electrifying because on one side of the church, people would be singing one verse of a song and across on the other side, others would be singing a second verse in response to the first one. What an experience that was. However, today, it appears as though we have become too rigid in the church. Although we don't always say it, our actions sometimes dictate to others that praising God "really don't take all of that." Even when the preacher is preaching a powerful message, some people just sit there as though he is not saying a word. There are some things that are completely prohibited in the Lord's house, but getting your praise on is just not one of them.

In this day and age, it appears as though we have way too many Secret Service agents in the church. Some of us have become too "proper" to verbally praise God. An even sadder reality is some of us won't even part our lips to say amen when we know the preacher is preaching truth. How sad is that? Our pastor reminds us all the time at the Bethel Church that the word *amen* is not a dirty word; it simply means, "I agree." So if you *know* the word and the preacher is preaching or teaching the word, then what prohibits you from saying amen? Too many times, we allow ourselves to become influenced by what's going on around us, allowing it to dictate our behavior in God's presence. The fact is God doesn't need any Secret Service agents. Instead, He is looking for those who will genuinely praise Him in spite of their surroundings.

The word of God declares in Luke 9:26 that if we are ashamed to own Him here on earth, then He will be ashamed to own us before His Father in Heaven. Who is willing to take such a risk? It is amazing how with one type of audience we want to be super saints, but then when the audience changes, we want to become part of the Secret Service. We must decide which side of the fence we are going to operate on because the Lord has made it crystal clear in Revelation 3:15–17 that being a lukewarm Christian makes Him sick! Therefore, I encourage you today to examine yourself and be very sure of which side of the fence you are standing on because God in not interested in having Secret Service agents, but He delights in those who are part of the CIA (Christians in Action).

Sharpening the Countenance of My Friend
(Proverbs 27:17)

Many people, much like myself, have experienced the agonizing emotional, mental, and financial discord that separation and divorce brings, all because what started out as a *Little House on the Prairie* has somehow evolved into a *Nightmare on Elm Street*! It seemed as though one day you were living a life that most would love to live, and then all of a sudden, something happened and things came crashing down, leaving you with a million questions and no answers. The love has somehow turned to hate. The trust that once existed has now been eroded like sand on a beach. The children are angry without a cause, and of course, the finances are suffering, all because somebody has opted to do his or her *own thing*! It seems like just yesterday, you were lovingly exchanging vows before a preacher and hundreds of guests, but now, all of a sudden, you are angrily exchanging words before a judge and a bunch of strangers! How many of us are honest enough to admit that it wasn't the wedding that got us but the marriage? But that's neither here nor there, because now the "Thrill Is Gone," there's no "Love or Happiness," and you are fighting for "Your Last Two Dollars"! Many years ago, this was my story. However, because of past challenges, I now fully understand Proverbs 22:6 in its entirety. Although we have all made decisions that were not fully reflective of our upbringing, the beautiful thing about the word of God is once it has been deposited within you, a withdrawal can be made at any time. When God delivers us from something, it becomes our responsibility to reach back and help others gain their deliverance through the sharing of our testimony. That's iron sharpening iron!

I love the fact that God is the chief vindicator and He does see everything—the good, the bad, and the ugly. My daughter, who is now a young woman, was a tiny two-month-old when my experience began. So precious, tiny, and innocent, she had no idea of the hell that had broken loose around her. When a marriage ends, it is strictly the fault of both persons involved. However, it affects everything and everybody around it. Things are said and done purely out of spite. Finances are withheld to prove a point, and ultimately the children become the casualties of a war they never even asked to be a part of. They suffer the most. I thank God every day for my family because they were the ones who were my iron through it all. There were times I didn't have a dime for diapers, but God provided. There were times I didn't have money for milk, but God provided. There were even times I couldn't pay day care, but an angel named Rose Bell kept my baby anyway and never let her go hungry. When God deems you to be victorious, no devil in hell can stop it!

When I discovered that I was in the battle of my life, it was precisely at that point that I began to reach deep within to reconnect with my biblical foundation, and you must find the strength to do the same. What was deposited in me early on in life is ... *prayer works,* and as I began to sincerely pray about my situation, things quickly changed for the better. The elders used to say, "If you trust and never doubt ... He will surely bring you out," and I know this to be true from my own personal experiences. If you are in a situation that is getting uglier by the minute, before you do anything, I encourage you to invite the Lord in. Go before Him, and tell the truth about where things are and the role you played in contributing to them. God requires transparency, and He demands honesty. I encourage you to ask Him to help you release all bitterness. I encourage you to ask Him to help you forgive your offender, and if necessary, ask for forgiveness if *you* are the offender. Many have passed through these waters, and God has seen them through, so never think that you are alone.

God sees your tears, and He knows the depth of your pain. Whatever you need, God is willing and able to provide it, but you must ask for it. Keep in mind that God does not always bring you out of a storm; sometimes He deems it necessary to teach you how to have peace while in the storm. While God does forgive us of our wrongs, I do need to inform you that there are consequences for our every action and only God knows how long the consequential phase will last. However, while you are in this phase, it is critical that you develop and maintain the spirit of humility, because the

Bible teaches us in James 4:6 that "God resists the proud, but He gives grace to the humble."

I am praying abundant blessings and great favor for you while you are on your journey to healing and wholeness in Jesus's name.

Standing in the Storm
(Isaiah 59:19)

In June 2001, Tropical Storm Allison inundated the Houston area with raging floodwaters. Developed from a tropical wave in the northern Gulf of Mexico, this storm drifted northward and then without warning, turned back to the south and reentered the Gulf, causing billions of dollars in damage. One day, the sun was shining brightly, and then just like that, the entire city became a river! Buses, eighteen-wheelers, and cars alike were all underwater. The military sent boats into neighborhoods to rescue people stranded on rooftops to carry them to safety. Blackhawk helicopters had to make emergency landings in unheard-of places, all for the common goal of getting people to safety. According to the National Weather Service, the consistent torrential downpour produced over forty inches of rain throughout the entire city. My parents, along with countless others, lost just about everything they spent their entire lives working to build. Life as they knew it had changed forever. It didn't matter whether you lived in the exclusive gated community or the projects; everybody was in the same boat (literally). Then, all of a sudden, the rain stopped. The floodwaters receded, and the time had come to survey all the damage. It was official. The utterly devastated city of Houston looked like a complete war zone!

Have you ever experienced a Tropical Storm Allison moment in your personal life? You know, the kind where the devil rushes in out of nowhere and with no warning, takes over your life like a raging flood? Has your life ever been devastated by one experience or telephone call? Have you ever been flying high with all cylinders humming in sync one day only to experience the total opposite the very next? All of a sudden, your marriage has been derailed like a runaway train. The kids have gone crazy! The boss is on your last nerve! Those you thought were friends are showing you *another side*. Because of one situation, the money is now funny and the change is now strange. As odd as it may sound, this really is a good time to rejoice in the Lord!

The Bible teaches us in James 1 that we are to count it all joy when we are faced with various trials, knowing that the trying of our faith will produce patience in our lives. God's divine purpose for tests and trials is to make us strong as well as expose what's really going on in our hearts. Sometimes life catches us off guard with situations that seem to work against us. But do they really? Isaiah 59:19b states, "When the enemy comes in like a flood, the Spirit of the Lord shall lift up a standard against him." God's word is that standard, and every time you speak it and marinate it in faith, not only do you build a fortress around yourself, but you strip Satan of his power. When we as believers learn to speak what we believe and not what we feel, we will really begin to make a spiritual impact in our own lives as well as in the lives of others. Life is about seasons, and this may be your storm season. I know without a doubt what storm seasons are like because when my father passed, for me, that was one storm. However, when my mother passed four short months later, I felt as though the same storm decided to turn back and reenter my life, just like Allison did the city of Houston back in 2001. But I had to activate my faith by reaching past my emotions to speak the word of God over my life and the lives of my siblings to help us through the very difficult period. I speak from sheer experience when I say that God is faithful and He honors His word. Hebrews 13:8 declares that He is the same yesterday, today, and forevermore, and just as He parted the Red Sea for the children of Israel to provide them a way of escape, He will surely do the same for you.

I encourage you today to take your focus off the situation and put it on the Savior, knowing that He is, has always been, and will continue to be a very present help in the time of trouble.

Standing Physically ... Kneeling Spiritually
(Matthew 18:19)

In life, we are constantly bombarded by challenges. Someone once said, "If it ain't one thing, it's another." However, I beg to differ. My philosophy is if it ain't one thing, it's ten, because personally, I am way past that luxurious stage of having to juggle just one or two challenges at a time. But no complaints here because multiple challenges come with the territory of growing stronger in your faith! You see, when we ask God to strengthen us in certain areas of our walk with Him, we in essence invite challenges into our lives. Challenges make us stronger. They make us wiser. They make us better. They strengthen our resolve. It is not enough to talk about what the word says; we must have it in our hearts. When it comes to our faith, our heads, our hearts, and our mouths *must* be in alignment with what God's word says. I stand on the word of God, but I kneel to the God of the word! I don't seek people's sympathy when I am faced with multiple challenges, but I do seek their partnership in prayer. Why? Because there is great power in agreement. The Lord says in Matthew 18:19, "Again, I say to you that if two of you agree on earth concerning anything that they ask, it will be done for them by my Father in Heaven."

Saints, opportunities don't always present themselves for us to stop and physically kneel in prayer. However, the posture of your body is not nearly as critical as the posture of your heart! God hears and answers sincere prayers. When the pressures of life come against me in an attempt to weigh me down, regardless of where I am, I get quiet and petition the Lord for clarity on what to do. Sometimes, in the office, I am standing right in the face of a known enemy and praying all at the same time. I stand simply because first I kneel. Depending on the situation, when the enemy comes in like a flood against me, I simply step back and allow the Lord to lift up a standard against him on my behalf (Isaiah 59:19). God's standard is His word. If it is a challenge of *fear*, I remind myself that God did not give me a spirit of fear but one of power, love, and a sound mind (2 Timothy 1:7). If it is a challenge of *faith*, I remind myself that without faith, it is impossible for me to please God, and if I am going to petition God for anything, I must first believe that He is able to handle the request (Hebrews 11:6). If it is a challenge of *forgiving others*, I remind myself that if I don't forgive those who have wronged me, then my Father in Heaven won't forgive me of my sins (Matthew 6:14). It's pretty simple, but in order to speak the word in faith, you must first know it and then you must apply it! You cannot be just a hearer of the word, you must become a doer of it (James 1:22). God has an excellent track record, and as you are faced with greater challenges, you will come to know that for yourself. It is never too late to strengthen your faith muscles. Regardless of where you are now, I encourage you to begin developing your faith in the Lord. God's word is His bond. Now is the time to let it become yours! I assure you, you will not be able to stand unless you first kneel.

The Church Ain't No Library

(Psalm 107:1–6)

As a child in elementary school, I remember going on many field trips with my class. Two of the most exciting places to go, in my opinion, were the zoo and the library. Even as a little person, I was always intrigued by all the knowledge that could be found in both places. I love the zoo (even to this day) because being in the domain of all the many different kinds of animals and having a firsthand glimpse into their world captivates my mind, and I love the library for the exact same reason. With countless books on countless subjects, the library can provide any interested person with answers on any given subject of his or her choice. However, there was one thing I must admit I never liked about being in the library, and that was the rule of always having to remain quiet and not disturb others. Oh, how I disliked this! Being in an environment where you are challenged to become excited about learning while at the same time being forced to put a cap on your excitement while you learn is just plain crazy to me. Stay with me, saints, 'cause I'm going somewhere ...

In Psalm 107, the writer is encouraging the reader to give thanks unto the Lord for He is good and because His mercy endures forever. The writer further encourages those of us who have been redeemed from the hand of the enemy by this great and powerful Lord to say so. Just like the library, the Holy Bible is chock-full of helpful information on every subject to invoke excitement within the heart and mind of the reader when he or she reads it. However, way too many Christians treat the church like a library when it comes time to making some noise. When you have been delivered from some stuff, you ought to have a praise that is powerful enough to shake the shingles on the most well-built church house! Whether it's in your dance, the clapping of your hands, or your war cry, when it comes to being delivered, you ought to make some noise! Every devil in hell ought to be able to hear your victory praise! In the words of my husband and pastor, "If people who share the pew with you in church got a problem with the way you praise God ... send out an SOS by telling them to *scoot over some*! If they still have a problem with it, then send out an SOSM by telling them to *scoot over some more!*"

Saints, never let anybody cause you to water down your praise for a God who has reached down and snatched you from Satan's grip! Each Sunday, as you prepare to enter into the house of worship, enter in boldly. Enter in ready for a crazy praise! Enter in with praise on your lips and thanksgiving in your heart! You have been delivered, and the very person you may be sitting next to may be anticipating his or her breakthrough, so why not give him or her an up-close-and-personal preview of how he or she may react when that breakthrough breaks through?

Remember, saints, it's all right to make some noise 'cause after all, the church ain't no library!

The Good Storms
(Romans 14:10–12)

One thing in life that is so perplexing to me is why it takes such a great catastrophe in order for people to realize that God does exist. Before Hurricane Sandy, there were Katrina, Rita, Ike, Allison, Carla, Felix, Gustav, and many others. And prior to each of these catastrophic storms, there has always been a great divide in the world. Whether racial, religious, political, educational, or socioeconomic, division has always been present, affecting everything and everybody in its path. Sadly, it appears as though things have deteriorated so until people really believe that they are the driving force in all things. Just as with any other catastrophic event recorded in history, we see the same story seems to repeat itself once again. In this recurring story, people have lost everything and are mentally, emotionally, and financially devastated, but yet in the midst of it all, they gather enough energy to pull together in the spirit of humanity and oneness to assist their neighbors regardless of race, religion, or political beliefs. But what happens when the storm clouds pass and the sun begins to shine again? You guessed it; the same divisive behaviors and attitudes of indifference are back to work just as they were prior to the storm.

So why are people so prone to usurp power and control over others simply because they are different? Why must people argue over differences rather than embrace them? When catastrophe strikes, does it really matter who is black or who is white or who is Democrat or who is Republican? Arguing over differences destroys us, but embracing them strengthens us. Why must we be brought to ruins before we get it? Why is prayer only a priority in this nation when disaster strikes? God has consistently proven Himself to be all powerful, and I just cringe when I hear mainstream media and others casually toss around the term *Mother Nature*, as though she is the one with all the power. From Genesis to Revelation, God makes Himself known to any person who diligently seeks to know Him. In addition, He clearly explains all the intimate details of how He formed the world and everything in it. Whether or not you believe the record is totally up to you. However, the fact does remain that He is God and beside Him there is no other. It terrifies me that a one-thousand-mile-wide storm that paralyzed millions of people and crippled the entire Eastern seaboard all at the same time was still not enough for some to wake up and acknowledge that God does exist. What exactly is it going to take? While I respect the knowledge and competence of skilled meteorologists, I do beg to differ with them in that there is only one who has the real power to walk out on the raging seas and speak peace to a storm, causing the winds to die down and the waves to be still, and I assure you, it is *not* Mother Nature.

Philippians 2:10–11 (KJV) clearly states, "Every knee shall bow and every tongue must confess that Jesus Christ is Lord," and anybody who really knows Him knows that He is a keeper of His word.

The Healing Power of a Hymn
(Lamentations 3:22–24)

The year 2012 was indeed the most emotionally devastating for me to say the least. Both of my parents passed away just four months apart, and trying to recover was anything but easy. All throughout the year, my schedule was dominated by ruthless to-do lists of responsibilities that offered no option for giving up. It seemed as though every time I completed one thing and thought I could breathe for a minute, three more things would miraculously appear. I found myself repeatedly reflecting on my days as a child and how I would love going to the park and hanging out on the merry-go-round. Constantly running here and there, picking up this, meeting about that, praying for this one, encouraging that one, typing this, and proofreading that left me in a mental fog on many occasions. But when things got to a certain point, I was so thankful that I always had a special place of escape. It is a park near my office. Just about every day, I would get the urge to drive over to it, park my car, and just sit quietly and listen. Oh how I love *this* park! It is filled with huge oak trees that provide a great place to soak up the shade while at the same time, enjoy an occasional breeze.

The first few minutes, I would just sit and collect myself and my thoughts as I watched the birds as they joyfully sang and flew … flew and sang. Then I would begin to hum in my spirit. "Oh to be kept by Jesus, kept by the power of God … kept through toils and trials, I am treading where Jesus had trod." Okay, then came the quiet exhale I had been longing for and needed so badly. Oh, how cleansing this was to the spirit and soul! I would then close my eyes and reflect on how grateful I was for having been kept by Jesus through all my difficult days. While I, to some degree, appreciate the contemporary sound of gospel music, there is just nothing like the soothing sound of an old hymn to usher my spirit into a place of intimate worship and rest with the Father.

So what kind of year have you had? Have you ever felt this way? For me, resting in the arms of Jesus is the purest form of rest. There is absolutely nothing that compares to spending quiet time with Him. When I am emotionally drained, He restores me. When my soul is thirsty, He refreshes me. When I am down, He is the lifter of my head. When I am in need of understanding, He downloads wisdom into my spirit. When I need to cry, He holds me and lovingly lets me. When I am hurt, He personally ministers to me. When I am afraid, He calms my every fear. In a nutshell, all I have ever needed, His hands have provided, and for that, I declare, "Great is Thy faithfulness." Is this your testimony? It surely is mine.

Having a relationship with the Lord is the reason why I continue to press my way because "Through It All," I have indeed learned to trust in Jesus. Betrayal of trust, job loss, marital struggles, deaths of loved ones ... you name it and I can still sing with joy in my heart, "Oh, to be kept by Jesus," for He has truly kept me. I tell ya, the Lord is a promise keeper and a way maker. Just when I think I am at the end of my rope, He grants me a divine extension every time and He will surely do the same for you. There is just nothing like being in the presence of the Most High God.

If you ever feel like you are spiraling out of control emotionally, mentally, or even spiritually, I invite you to get into the presence of the Lord. If you need assistance, just ask Him. I assure you He will answer. When the storms of life begin to rage in my life, He has truly proven that He will "Stand by Me." And yes, when waves of affliction sweep over my soul and sunlight is hidden from view, if ever I am tempted to fret or complain, all I have to do is just "Think of His Goodness."

Saints, there is still "A Bright Side Somewhere," and today, I encourage you not to stop until you find it, because I assure you, you have way more to be thankful for than you have to complain about.

The Irony of Life
(Psalm 46:10)

What do you do when it seems like life is serving you up way more than you can handle? You be still and trust God. How about when you have way more questions than you have answers? You be still and trust God. Or better yet, when you are challenged by multiple situations that seem to be winning in the race for your sanity? Yes, you be still and trust God. Trusting God is not something that happens overnight. Instead, learning to trust God is a process that is personally escorted in by challenging situations you have absolutely no ability to control. After all, if we could control them, then would there be no need for God and would we really grow?

A man for whom I have great respect and admiration, Dr. Walter Hanks Jr. (Pastor Emeritus of the Promised Land Church of Houston, Texas), said something so very profound as he was preaching his wife's home-going celebration. He said to the standing-room-only crowd of people, "I am a pretty perceptive person, yet I didn't see this one coming!" Oh my, how this statement impacted my spirit! He was in essence saying that the passing of his dearly beloved wife of forty-six years was so totally unexpected. And that's the irony of life … One day, we're all laughing together and enjoying one another as the chain of life seems strong and unbreakable, and then all of a sudden, a break occurs! Not only is it a break, but a major link. Immediately the chain is weakened. So what do you do when this happens? You be still and trust God.

I do not encourage you to do anything that I have not done myself. I do not share fictitious stories, but I share life. I share my life. I have no concern for those who gossip about what I share with the world, because encouraging others is my ministry. My ministry *is* my life. My ministry is to the world. The irony is that I never in a million years would have imagined that I would be partnering with such a powerful vessel in ministry as in the person of my husband. I never in a million years would have imagined that I would have become pregnant and abort a baby. Never in a million years would I have imagined that after finally settling down and saying, "Yes, Lord" to the wonderful life He already had predestined for me, that I would miscarry two babies in five months and not be a basket case. And God knows I never in a million years would have imagined having to bury my mother four months after my father ... all in the same year. However, each of these emotionally devastating situations has taught me how to be still and trust God. Sometimes God will provide you with a glimpse of why, simply because when you can press past *your* pain to help others through theirs, God is pleased.

The irony of life was to support my sister-friend Reta as she suffered in silence when her mother passed just two short months after my mother passed. The irony of life is sharing the very precious moment with members of our church family who went into premature labor at five months and lost both of their twin daughters. To watch two little angels of God enter this world, each no larger than a soda can is amazingly tough. Pastor and I cried with them, and we prayed with them. With absolutely no words of explanation, we simply had to quietly remind them that God is still God and He is still good.

As I minister to people, I share with them that it is not on the mountaintop that we grow. Instead, it's in the valley. You see, in the valley, many tears are shed. In the valley, there is great heartache. In the valley, there is overwhelming pain and suffering, but in the valley, there is God and in the midst of it all, saints, we must be still and know that He is God.

Towers of Heaven

(2 Corinthians 4:7–10)

At one point in time, I probably had the absolute worst-looking, most beat-up, beat-down, taped-up, and tattered cell phone in the whole world— or Houston at least! God bless the women of the Bethel Missionary Baptist Church. They were constantly saying, "Sister McCray, this phone is just ridiculous! We are going to get you a new one because we don't want our pastor's wife walking around with a cell phone that has Scotch tape on the back of it holding it together" ... Gotta love them (and God knows I do)! One, bless her heart, had even given me a really pretty Blackberry with a sleek, up-to-date body style, but as fate and Verizon would have it, it did not connect with my AT&T service. After hearing this for the umpteenth time, I finally said to them, "Look, my phone works! When I need to make a call, I can, and when I need to receive a call, I can! What if the Lord replaced us simply because we no longer looked pleasing to Him?"

Now really, people, how many of us are perfect every day from the inside out? Has anybody, other than me, of course, been beat up, beat down, and tattered by life? Troubled on every side to the point of needing the word of God to stick with us for the sole purpose of holding it all together? It does not matter how well put together we are on the outside; if we are not connecting with the right service, we are still messed up on the inside. Having said that, I am so thankful that no matter how distressed I may appear to be on the outside, my divine purpose remains the same on the inside. And because I choose to obediently walk in my divine purpose, the Towers of Heaven always hear me when I call needing help.

The beautiful thing is the God I serve is an on-time God. Yes He is! He is so wise that He never gets my call mixed up with anybody else's, and studying His word helps to raise my bars for extreme clarity and connection every time. I thank God for the elders teaching me that Jesus really is on the main line and that I can always call Him and tell Him what I want. When sick, I call Him. When in trouble, I call Him. When lonely, I call Him. When financially challenged, I call Him. No gas in the car? I call Him. When the bills are due, I call Him. When battling with the enemy, I call Him. When the marriage is rocky, I call Him. When the children decide to go crazy, I call Him. When challenged on the job, I call Him. When emotionally drained, I call Him. When my daddy died, I called Him. Four months later, when my mama died, I called Him. When I am angry, I call Him. When hurt, I call Him. Battling with depression, I call Him. Struggling with not feeling good enough, I call Him. When my faith is shaky, I call Him. For any and all reasons, I call on God, and guess what. You can too.

Regardless of the time of day or the nature of the challenge, God is on call twenty-four hours a day, seven days a week, and He is waiting to hear from you. You are indeed special to Him, and He loves you dearly. Saints, don't let the devil rob you by causing you to believe anything else. I've got just two little questions for you. Can you hear me now? Or better yet, is He your world delivered? As always, if anybody knows, you do.

Too Grateful to Be Hateful
(Philippians 4:8)

Did you know that it takes way more energy to hate than to love? Did you know that it takes twice as many muscles to frown as it does to smile? Did you know that a person can read you without ever asking you a single question? Did you know that your words are seeds? Did you know that there is only one thing that the enemy is really after and that is your mind? Each of these very simple but thought-provoking questions is being raised to assist you in taking a personal inventory of where you are at this juncture on your journey called life. Sometimes we operate on autopilot without even realizing it, but I guarantee you other people see it. People study us whether we realize it or not. Having said that, what lessons are you teaching today? Are you teaching from an open book or a closed mind? Do your lessons come from a grateful heart or a hateful heart?

It is easily recognizable when you are grateful as well as when you are hateful. Both of these characteristics have the power to leave a lasting impression on others but in very opposite ways. Gratefulness adds, but hatefulness subtracts. Gratefulness multiplies, but hatefulness divides. Gratefulness draws, but hatefulness drives. Regardless of which side of the fence you are on at this very moment, you are there because of the sum total of your thoughts. Did you know that there is really only one thing that the enemy is after, and that is your mind? The reason why is simple. Satan knows the power of the mind (sometimes better than we do).

The Bible advises us in Proverbs 4:23 to guard our minds because out of the mind flows the issues of life. In other words, the mind is the epicenter of the entire operation. The mind is the nucleus for all activity. The mind is the focal point of everything that goes on. This is why it is so critical that we guard it. We must choose and handle our thoughts with extreme wisdom and care. This is most necessary because what we think produces what we say. What we say eventually produces what we do. What we do in essence shows the world who we really are. This goes back to my previous statement of people being able to read you without asking you a single question. All others need to do is look and listen. A grateful spirit produces kindness. A grateful spirit gives. A grateful spirit ignites joy within others. A grateful spirit is thankful regardless of the situation. Now, of course, there are situations and challenges that present themselves and cause us to react because we are human. However, once again, that is the beauty of the human mind. The mind has the ability to recalibrate or reboot itself. If you need to know what's really going on in your life, check your thoughts. Pay closer attention to what you are thinking and why you are thinking what you are thinking.

As you read this passage, I use the same words as penned by the apostle Paul in his letter to the Philippian church to encourage you. "Finally, brethren, whatsoever things are true, whatsoever things are honest, whatsoever things are just, whatsoever things are pure, whatsoever things are lovely, whatsoever things are of good report; if there be any virtue, and if there be any praise, think on these things" (Philippians 4:8 KJV).

Are you living in the mansion of gratefulness or on a remote island of hatefulness? If you are unsure in any way, check your thoughts because they hold the key to the truth.

Too Many Babies in the Church

(1 Corinthians 3:1–3)

A couple of years ago, I had a conversation with my sister regarding my nephew AJ, whom I call "Biscuit," and she was sharing with me that she was about to start him on stage 1 baby foods. I was so excited that he was finally about to add some meat to his diet, and lo and behold, the Lord spoke a word! In my quiet time, I began to wonder just how much of an impact the church would have on the world if believers would begin consuming the meat of the word as opposed to milk only. Milk runs through you, but meat sticks to you. Remaining on spiritual milk is a choice people make simply because they don't want the responsibility that comes with consuming the meat of the word. Others remain on milk because they don't want to be held accountable for what they learn. Then there are those who are just plain lazy and have no excuse at all. Now please understand me when I say, I am not referring to new converts who must start out on the milk of the word. I am, however, referring to the longtime milk drinkers who clearly should be on solid meat as long as they have been in the church. They are easily recognizable by their actions. They politic for positions, constantly display bad attitudes, and are deceptive and treacherous without a second thought. Need I go further, or did you get the point? On the contrary, when you have graduated to consuming the meat of God's word, your attitude will begin to change for the better. Your life will become transformed as your mind is renewed through word. People will love seeing you come as opposed to seeing you go.

Years ago, my husband preached a message entitled, "Too Many Babies in the Church," and I tell you, it made some people downright angry. But to be angry would suggest that possibly they were still very much on a milk diet. Hebrews 4:2 states, "For the word of God is living and powerful, and sharper than any two-edged sword, piercing even to the division of soul and spirit, and of joints and marrow, and is a discerner of the thoughts and intents of the heart." So believe me when I say God knows if you are on milk or meat because He knows what's in your heart.

God knows your spiritual diet better than you do. It has been said—and it is true—that whatever is going on down on the inside will show up on the outside. Now, the reality is there are some milk drinkers who appear to be meat eaters. However, the truth is always revealed when an annual day or celebration rolls around, and they are not appointed to serve as chairperson or are not asked to work with a committee. You can only hide for so long, and then God will cause the truth to be revealed. Whether it's anger, bitterness, secret hatred, jealousy, envy, low self-esteem, or any other secret issue going on in your life, you must understand that the eyes of the Lord are in every place, beholding the evil and the good. In other words, God sees it all! The apostle Paul in his first letter to the Corinthian church, so eloquently puts it this way: "When I was a child, I spake as a child, I understood as a child, I thought as a child: but when I became a man, I put away childish things" (1 Corinthians 13:11 KJV). Saints, it's time to put away childish thoughts and behaviors because they have absolutely no place in the house of God. This crippling behavior does far more harm than good and can be spiritually debilitating to a new believer, which will surely not please God. If this is you, confess it to God, ask His forgiveness, and repent (or turn away) from this behavior. Remember the Holy Spirit is about conviction and conversion. He is not about condemnation. Each of us at one time or another has been on milk, but the difference is some of us have decided to hunger and thirst after more spiritually and have chosen to graduate to receiving the meat of the word.

Today, I encourage you to make a decision. Which one will it be, milk or meat? Remember the choice is yours.

Toxic Temptation
(John 10:10 and 1 Corinthians 10:13)

Temptation. It's something we all deal with. It's something none of us are above. It's even something that all of us *think* about way more than we care to admit. Before we go further, let's be crystal clear about the subject matter. Now keep in mind, we are not just talking temptation; we are talking *toxic* temptation. I am certain you would agree with me when I say that the description of the temptation alone is a game changer. Temptation comes in many forms and disguises itself in many ways. It can range from something as simple and as innocent as going against the diet and taking another cookie out of the jar to as toxic as going against the word of God and grabbing a *cookie* out of someone else's jar (you'll catch that in a minute). Before any of us fall prey to the temptation of becoming self-righteous, let me remind us of what Romans 3:23 says. It plainly states, "For all have sinned and fall short of the glory of God." The field should be leveled quite nicely by now because the word of God just reminded us that everybody has been guilty of something. Now, let's delve into our discussion.

What is so intriguing about temptation? Is it the idea of getting something that we know we shouldn't have? Is it the idea of being able to conquer something (or someone) that appears to be unconquerable? Or is it an outside manifestation of expression relative to something that's really haunting us on the inside? Actually, it can be one of these, two of these, or all of these. Contrary to what most people may think, toxic temptation is not just about sex, lies, and videotape. I say this simply because when the topic is mentioned, that is the first thing that most people tend to think. However, toxic temptation can actually be about a bad friendship or relationship. It can be about overspending. It can even be about overindulging in all the wrong foods. Temptation simply means to desire something bad, but when you place the *toxic* label on it, you just caused it to become deadly.

There are things that once tempted me in the past that don't even warrant a second thought today. However, please understand that old temptations are always replaced with new and improved temptations. Have you ever heard the saying "new level ... new devil"? Okay, that's what I mean. So before all the celebrations begin, let me inform you that Satan never gives up. In fact, John 10:10 states, "The thief cometh not, but for to steal, and to kill, and to destroy." Simply put, Satan is not trying to play with you. Instead, he and his imps are out to destroy you and worse—*kill* you! Satan has a blueprint on every believer, and yes, he does know how you have matured in the word, yet he still persists. He knows what you like. He knows how you like what you like. He even knows how you like what you like served up the way you like it. And he definitely knows when you are in a vulnerable place in your life. Don't dare get it twisted; he is truly a force to be reckoned with. But God is able! Only the word of God is powerful enough to handle Satan and his kingdom. This is yet another reason why it is so critical that we read and study the word of God for ourselves, as we are reminded in 2 Timothy 2:15. You need to be able to fight—and the only way you can fight and defeat Satan is through the word of God.

One way Satan attempts to defeat us is through our thoughts. Sometimes when we are struggling with a particular issue or temptation, Satan will lead us to believe that we are the only ones fighting the fight, but it is not so. First Corinthians 10:13 (KJV) informs us, "There hath no temptation taken you but such as is common to man: but God is faithful, who will not suffer you to be tempted above that ye are able; but will with the temptation also make a way to escape, that ye may be able to bear it." Thank God for the word because it still has the power. It does not matter what you are struggling with, somebody else has gone through the exact same thing. In order to overcome toxic temptation, I strongly encourage you to seek wisdom from the word of God on whatever issue you are struggling with. As you consistently do this and you position yourself to hear from God, you will discover that the Holy Spirit will lead you in the direction of other saints who can help you fight the good fight of faith. There is power in agreement, and when you have true prayer warriors standing in the gap for you, it produces great strength for your journey.

Toxic temptation—it may look good, and it may even be packaged just right. However, if you unwrap it, I assure you the effects can be catastrophic in every way possible. Therefore, when it slithers your way, it will do you well simply to respond, "Thanks but no thanks" in Jesus's name.

Unnecessary Roughness
(Ezekiel 7:4)

Have you ever heard the term *unnecessary roughness*? Any real sports fanatic can tell you quite a bit about this call. This is a term that is commonly used to bring attention to the mistreatment of another while on the playing field or court. This behavior can be accompanied by stiff penalties if witnessed by the referee. Unfortunately, this call can be used in the church as well. We see it all the time from the pulpit to the pews. We see it in the choir. We see it with the ushers. We see it with the deacons. We see it in the mission. We see it in the youth department. I could go on, but the point is wherever you have people, you have the propensity for *unnecessary roughness* to take place. When a person is being unnecessarily rough with others, sometimes it is the result of an internal issue taking place on the inside of the perpetrator. However, none of us has the right to mistreat others. I myself have been guilty of this, and believe me, the penalty is stiff, because the eyes of the *referee* are in every place, beholding the evil and the good, according to Proverbs 15:3. In the football arena, the guilty party can cause the team to lose yardage, thus giving the opposing team a definite advantage. Well, it works the same way in the church. When we are guilty of *unnecessary roughness* toward other believers, we set the church back, and depending on our position on the field of salvation, this could give Satan a perfect opportunity to score a touchdown by causing the offended party to completely walk away from the faith.

So what types of acts constitute an *unnecessary roughness* call? Let's discuss a few. Are you aware of the fact that when you have an ugly attitude with people, that constitutes unnecessary roughness? Mean-mugging people ... unnecessary roughness! Plotting and scheming against one another ... unnecessary roughness! Unforgiveness ... unnecessary roughness! Lying on people ... unnecessary roughness! Slandering other people's names ... unnecessary roughness! Defaming someone's reputation and character ... unnecessary roughness! The Bible reminds us in Ezekiel 7:4 that the Lord will not look on you with pity; He will not spare you. He will surely repay you for your conduct and for the detestable practices you have committed. He further assures, "Then you will know that I am the Lord." My God, my God! The next time you are even thinking about committing an act that goes against the divine playbook, I encourage you to remember the word of the Lord because He is the ultimate judge and He has the power to press the replay tape for you to see your own deeds—not anybody else's deeds but yours. Once the deed has been done, the *unnecessary roughness* call will be made against you, and after further review, the fourth and final step is the issuing of the penalty. The question is, can you handle the call once it is made?

Weapon of Mass Destruction
(Isaiah 54:17)

Did you know that Satan has a weapon of mass destruction for the believer? Just in case you don't know what it is, let me enlighten you. Satan's weapon of mass destruction for the believer is *fear*—fear of the unknown, fear of rejection, fear of failure, fear of success, fear of not being loved, fear of growing old alone, fear of loneliness, and even fear of fear! However, God's weapon against all fear is faith. Secrets are the common thread that connects every type of fear. Reason being is because almost all secrets are rooted in dark places. Secrets are those classified pieces of information we carefully conceal because we believe that if others found out about them, they would immediately begin to view us in a different light. Secrets break up marriages. Secrets destroy friendships. Secrets break fellowship. Secrets isolate. Secrets violate. Secrets desecrate. People will do anything and everything within their power to keep a secret hidden.

The Bible teaches us in John 8:32 that the only way the believer can experience freedom is by walking in truth. However, Satan has a way of infiltrating the thoughts of people, causing them to believe that they are the only ones guilty of committing a particular sin (isolation). Fear grips the mind, and holds the thoughts of a person hostage for the purpose of self-destruction. In other words, fear is a stronghold. However, the Bible teaches us in 2 Corinthians 10:3–5 that the weapons of our warfare are not carnal but mighty through God to the pulling down of strongholds. Saints, Satan knows that with God's help, you have the power to overcome his debilitating grip on your mind. He knows that death and life are in the power of your tongue. (But do *you* know that?) He knows that when you get the word down on the inside, you can speak to your situations with authority so that no weapon he forms against you will be able to prosper. (But again, do *you* know that?) Satan knows that God will never leave you nor forsake you. (But do *you* know that?) Satan knows that God will always be your very present help in the time of trouble. (But do *you* know that?) You are no match for Satan. However, when you submit yourself to God and resist Satan, the Bible says in James 4:7 that he must flee from you. Word of advice ... Don't ever try to handle Satan on your own, because I assure you, the results can and will leave you wounded beyond your absolute wildest imagination.

There is not a person walking the face of this earth who has not messed up! How can I be so sure? Because Romans 3:23 (KJV) declares, "All have sinned and fall short of the glory of God." So there you have it. If you ever hear people boldly state that they are without sin, please remind them of this passage. I have made many mistakes in my life. However, I do know that no person can condemn me, according to Romans 8:1. Granted, others may not have done what you did, but they are guilty of having done something. All unrighteousness is sin, and God hates all sin. However, the key to overcoming sin is going boldly to the throne of grace, laying out the facts before the Lord in the spirit of true repentance, and allowing Him to deal with the situation as He cleans you up in the process.

It really does not matter if you are an educated scholar, president and CEO of a Fortune 500 Company, the pastor of one of the largest churches in America, or just a single parent trying to make ends meet. Everyone has wrestled with the enemy in his or her lifetime. It is because of my valley experiences that I can say with strong conviction that I know God is faithful and just to forgive you and cleanse you from all unrighteousness through His word. Yes, it is my valley experiences that have taught me that God really will be your strong tower against the enemy. There were many times in my life when I felt as though the enemy was winning the battle, but then, just like in a good novel, God always comes through in the end and defeats the bad guy. God is real. I am so glad that He goes before me and makes the crooked paths straight for me to follow. Therefore, because He is no respecter of person, I encourage you to go before Him and release those secret sins that are causing you to decay from the inside out. God will indeed give you beauty for your ashes. He's just waiting on you to come forward and make the exchange, but you must be willing to give it all to Him. It is then that in the grand scheme of things, He will give you a garment of praise in exchange for that spirit of heaviness you have been carrying for so many years all because of those secret sins.

God is real, and I personally invite you to taste and see for yourself that He really is good.

When You Function under the Unction
(Proverbs 18:16)

I clearly recall when the Lord instructed me to walk in my gift. The date was August 18, and the year was 2012. It was exactly eight days (eight represents new beginnings) after my father's death. It was the day of his funeral to be exact. We made it through the funeral, and Mom seemed to be doing okay. People and food were everywhere, and silence was such a rare and distant pleasure at the time. I felt like something was cutting off my wind. I desperately sought a private place just to quiet myself and breathe. When I found it, my breath returned almost instantly. Then the Lord began to speak. I am so thankful that I know the voice of God in my life because when life becomes overwhelming, His voice is one I never have to question. The divine conversation began with Him instructing me to walk in my gift. I said to Him, "Lord, what are you referring to? I need you to show me what it is." Days passed … no answer from God. A week passed … no answer from God. Two weeks passed … no answer from God. Then finally on Saturday, September 8, I had a dream. God clearly used this dream to answer my prayer. The dream took me back to my third-grade awards program, held at the end of each school year at Robert L. Frost Elementary School in Houston, Texas. My entire family was present for this great occasion. I remembered being all dressed up in my Sunday morning church clothes as I, along with all the other third-graders, were being shuffled onto the stage like little cattle. The cafeteria was filled with excitement as many family members armed with Polaroid cameras, complete with blinding flashes, were perched and ready to snap a picture of their little ones as they went up to receive their award. Immediately, I knew God had indeed answered my prayer, because it was at this assembly program that I received the first-place blue ribbon for winning the writing contest for the entire third grade. Good God Almighty, just like that, I knew then that God had revealed to me my area of giftedness, and boy was I excited!

Proverbs 18:16 declares that a person's gift will make room for him or her and bring him or her before great people. However, before you claim this promise, you must first operate in your gift, and in order to operate in your gift, you must first know what your gift is. Prior to you entering into your mother's womb, God had a plan and a purpose for your life, according to Jeremiah 29:11. In addition, 1 Corinthians 12 lets us know that every person has been given at least one spiritual gift for the purpose of helping to build up and strengthen the body of Christ. In order to know what your spiritual gift is, you must pray and ask the Lord to reveal it to you. Now, just because you do something well does not mean that it is your spiritual gift, and if you don't know what yours is, don't be discouraged. Just keep asking the Lord. For some people, it may take years of listening, and for others, the answer may come instantly, but this one thing I know for sure: He will answer you. When He reveals it, the time comes for you to begin walking in it. Your gift may be faith or wisdom or healing, or maybe it's to prophecy, but whatever it is, you must use it to the glory of God. When your gift glorifies God and edifies the body of Christ, He will cause it to make room for you and bring you before great people. There are many gifted and talented people in this world, but it is the anointing of the Holy Spirit that makes the difference. When you are anointed by the Lord, He uses your gift not only to touch people's lives but to minister to their souls.

There are great rewards that await you when you function under the unction. When you function under the unction, you are no longer in control. Instead, you are being guided by the Holy Spirit as you operate under His mighty power, knowing that it is the anointing that breaks the yoke and destroys every stronghold. When you function under the unction, the spirit of the Lord will cause opportunities to overtake you. When you function under the unction, He will enlarge your territory. When you function under the unction, He'll cause even your greatest of enemies to be at peace with you. Yes, when you function under the unction, the Lord will dispatch angels to protect you from the snares of the enemy. When you function under the unction, He will cause you to sidestep every trap that the enemy strategically lays just for you. When you function under the unction, although calamity may be all around you, it will not come near you, according to Psalm 91. And yes, saints, when you function under the unction, the Lord is committed to watching over His word to perform it in every area of your life (Jeremiah 1:12 NLT).

Who Stopped the Music?
(Ecclesiastes 3:1)

Some time ago, I was chatting with a girlfriend who was excitedly talking about going to the Jill Scott concert in Houston. After our conversation, I began to think about my old party days. On Friday, Saturday, and Sunday nights, I would be on the dance floor moving and grooving to my favorite jam for what seemed like thirty minutes when all of a sudden something would unexpectedly happen that caused the record to scratch or skip a beat. Everything stopped. Everybody started looking around like "What happened?"

Well, guess what? That's exactly how life is! How often do we find ourselves moving and grooving through life only to have it unexpectedly skip a beat? Whether it's the loss of a job or a loved one, the ending of a marriage or relationship, or whatever the case may be, life happens! What do you do? How do you respond? Ecclesiastes 3 speaks about the seasons of life and how each season produces its fair share of change. The one thing that is constant in life is change. Not everybody handles change well. Some breeze through it while at the same time, others may struggle for a lifetime. But aren't you glad that God is all-wise and all-knowing? He knows exactly what we will face in this life, and before we can even tell Him how we feel, He stands ready, willing, and able to help us through it.

If you are in a season of change, tell God about it. One of the greatest things about talking to the Father is that we don't have to make sure we use proper English, nor will He turn a deaf ear because our sentence structure is not perfect. All each of us must have is a sincere heart.

Got some challenges in your life? Tell God about them, and allow Him put a new song in your heart that will surely cause you to move to a different beat.

Write the Vision
(Habakkuk 2:2–3)

I am proud to admit that I am a giver. Don't really need a reason. I just enjoy giving and sharing with others. One gift that I just absolutely love to give is a journal. Oh, how I love my journals! I keep one next to my bed and in each of the rooms that I frequent most in my home. I do this because I want to always be prepared when the Lord speaks to me. I also write when something or someone is heavy on my heart and mind or when I encounter a vision. I wonder sometimes how many people really know the importance of writing something down. Did you know that when you take the time to write something down, it greatly increases your chances of remembering what it is that you wrote? Pastor F. D. Sampson Sr. of Houston, Texas, always says, "A long pencil always beats a short memory," and this is so very true.

I am teased often because I make a list for everything. Regardless of where I am, I believe in keeping a list. For me, it serves two purposes—of course, it helps me to remember what needs to be done, but it also helps me to track my personal progress over time. However, it wasn't until about maybe fifteen years ago that I realized that it was actually a biblical instruction to write things down. In Habakkuk 2:2–3, the Lord instructs Habakkuk to write down his visions because his visions are a sneak preview of what's to come in the future. When you believe so strongly that something is going to come to pass in your life, it becomes necessary to write it down because you then have a timeline to refer back to when it does come to pass.

One Saturday afternoon while sitting in the emergency room with my daughter, I felt led to journal. After I completed my passage, I then began to casually flip back through the pages of journal entries regarding the details of my life down through the year. My eyes immediately halted when I got to a particular date. It was Saturday, May 12, 2012. What an awesome day that was! I was invited to pray the intercessory prayer of Thanksgiving at a prayer breakfast at the Galilee MBC that morning, and the Lord was indeed in the house. Months prior to the breakfast, I had been in an all-out battle with the enemy, and quite frankly, I was exhausted the day of the breakfast and was in desperate need of a breakthrough of my own. But how many of you know that God always has a ram in the bush? Here I am on program to pray for others and literally fighting the enemy for my own sanity all at the same time. But the Bible teaches us in Ephesians 6:8 that what we make happen for others, God will surely make happen for us. I was on the verge of my breakthrough and was too exhausted to even see it. I truly thank God for empowering me with the ability to hang on because just as the breakfast was nearing its end, there was a woman of God in the house who spoke a prophetic word over my life, regarding what was about to come to pass. Ooh, Jesus! Hallelujah to the Lamb of God! This was precisely what I had been waiting for. The Holy Spirit used her to speak directly to me! As I sat there reading over that particular journal entry, I began to feel such an excitement in my spirit all over again, simply because everything that was prophesied to me on that day had actually come to pass in my life. I thanked God for His goodness and mercy and for being a keeper of His word regarding fighting all my battles.

Saints, if ever you find yourself becoming weary in your faith as you wait on God, I encourage you to purchase a journal and write down your thoughts and feelings. If you have a dream or vision, write it down. If there is something that you would like to accomplish, write it down. But don't stop there … make absolutely sure you date it and time it! Doing this will provide you with an excellent boost of patience and hope when the next challenge comes along because you will have recorded victories to refer back to. One of the things I love most about God is that He does not show favoritism of any kind, according to Romans 2:11. If He did it for me, I know that He will surely do the same for you! Having said that … go ahead and write the vision; you will be glad you did! I know because you are actually reading one of mine.

Conclusion
Final Word ...

It is my sincere hope that your heart has been inspired and your spirit refreshed by the words that have been penned on these pages. Each of these short, easy-to-read parables was written specifically to encourage you to develop a closer walk and more intimate relationship with the Father. Many times, as Christians, we tend to be uptight and intimidated by the presence of God. However, we must remember that He *is* our heavenly Father. Not only that, but He loves us and always desires to spend quality time with us.

The divine purpose of this book was simply to help you understand that God is everywhere and that He can use anything or anybody to minister to your soul. However, this epiphany will never manifest until we release all the preconceived thoughts and ideas that we have about our heavenly Father. Knowing the Father intimately means spending precious quality time listening to, laughing with, and loving on Him just like a natural father. Remember the words of Ecclesiastes 3: "To everything there is a season."

I have one final word of encouragement for you. As you move forward and are faced with new challenges, before attempting to take matters into your own hands, I encourage you to do three things first: (1) quiet yourself, (2) meditate on God's promises, and (3) actively focus on His creation around you. As you do this, go ahead and release your cares to Him, and ask the Holy Spirit to minister to you. By doing this, I assure you that you will discover exactly what I discovered ... that He really is a *proven* bridge over troubled waters.

Printed in the United States
By Bookmasters